# WALKING WITH GOD

# WALKING WITH GOD

Martyn Lloyd-Jones

LIFE IN CHRIST ▫ VOLUME TWO

STUDIES IN 1 JOHN



CROSSWAY BOOKS
A DIVISION OF GOOD NEWS PUBLISHERS
WHEATON, ILLINOIS • CAMBRIDGE, ENGLAND

CREDO
PUBLISHING CORPORATION

*Walking with God*



First U.S. edition published 1993 by Crossway Books, a division of Good News Publishers, 1300 Crescent Street, Wheaton, Illinois 60187.

Published in association with Credo Books, P.O. Box 3175, Langley, B.C., Canada V3A 4R5.



Cover illustration: Keith Stubblefield

First printing, 1993

Printed in the United States of America

ISBN 0-89107-735-9

01 00 99 98 97 96 95 94 93
15 14 13 12 11 10 9 8 7 6 5 4 3 2 1

First British Edition 1993



ISBN 1 85684 051 4

Production and Printing in the United States of America for
CROSSWAY BOOKS
16 Glebe Road, Cambridge, England CB1 4SZ

# TABLE OF CONTENTS


| | | |
|---|---|---|
| | *Acknowledgements* | vii |
| 1 | Sin | 9 |
| 2 | Doctrine and Life | 21 |
| 3 | The Advocate | 33 |
| 4 | Knowing That We Know Him | 43 |
| 5 | Loving the Brethren | 55 |
| 6 | Children, Young Men, and Fathers | 67 |
| 7 | The Love of the World | 81 |
| 8 | The Antichrist | 93 |
| 9 | Of the Church | 105 |
| 10 | The Anointing of the Holy Spirit | 117 |
| 11 | The Truth and the Lie | 131 |
| | *Notes* | 143 |

# ACKNOWLEDGEMENTS

These sermons were first preached in Westminster Chapel in 1948/9 and form the sequel to *Fellowship with God.* Eagle-eyed readers will note that the last verse of chapter 2 is not dealt with. This is because the Doctor felt that that verse was better incorporated in the sermons on chapter 3, and so his exposition of verse 29 will appear as the first chapter of volume 3 of this series.

The basic editing of these sermons was carried out by Christopher Catherwood, the Doctor's eldest grandson and Editorial Director at Crossway Books in England. However, as usual, an enormous amount of work on these manuscripts has also been done by Elizabeth Catherwood, the Doctor's elder daughter and literary executrix, and to her go special thanks. (She has also done much unsung on many of his other books, so it is fitting that she should be given her due honour here.) As before, Alison Walley has not only copy edited the manuscript, but typed it onto disk for the publishers, and so full thanks are due to her as well.

Lastly, much of the vision for this series comes from the enthusiasm shown by J. I. Packer, who with his wife heard many of them preached back in the 1940's, and also to Lane Dennis, the publisher for Crossway, whose commitment to the cause of Christian truth has made their publication possible.

# 1
# Sin

My little children, these things write I unto you, that ye sin not. And if any man sin, we have an advocate with the Father, Jesus Christ the righteous: and he is the propitiation for our sins: and not for ours only, but also for the sins of the whole world.

1 JOHN 2:1-2

There are certain periods in our lives–New Year's Eve perhaps[1] or certain important occasions–when we find ourselves thinking about life itself, its whole object and meaning and purpose. We think about ourselves, wondering what we have made of life, what are we doing with it and what is the ultimate future that is very steadily facing us all. Probably, quite inevitably, we also look backwards, wondering how we have conducted and comported ourselves hitherto, and probably also we are all aware of a sense of dissatisfaction. We are aware that we have not done what we should have done and what we intended to do. We are aware of a sense of failure and inadequacy, and at the same time we are aware within us of a desire to do better in the days that lie ahead. Those are the thoughts that tend to come to us as we pause at any point in life and look backwards and forward, and perhaps the greatest and the most important thing of all is that we should be quite certain about life itself and its meaning and its purpose.

Now the danger at a time like this always is to take too superficial a view. The trouble, it seems to me, about New Year's and all our other resolutions is that they are resolutions with regard to particular things, but we fail to be concerned about first principles. Our danger is that we deal with the symptoms instead of with the disease, and that is surely the biggest danger as we look back and review the past. We tend to get down immediately to detail before we have really considered the big principles themselves, and thus it is that life so often tends to become rather futile.

One of the real difficulties in life is not to be mastered by it. We all tend inevitably to become victims of circumstances and chance and of accident and thus we go on from day to day perhaps feeling uneasy at times, feeling concerned and then somehow or other getting rid of that feeling or forgetting it, and so we are back where we were before. Then, perhaps, something big and important will take place; a birth, a death, an illness or an accident, some calamity which we read of in the newspapers, or war, something devastating, and again we are pulled up and we begin to think and to meditate. We are once more conscious of this sense of dissatisfaction and lack of ease about ourselves, and we ponder and propose that really something must be done about it. We are genuinely determined to do so and then, somehow or another, that acute state passes and in a few days we are back again exactly where we were at the beginning.

Now that, I suggest, is not an unfair or inadequate picture of the life of the average person; aware from time to time of something centrally wrong and then being confined only to detail instead of to the central thing. And the inevitable result is that the main tenor of life continues more or less as it was before and nothing really vital has been changed.

Now the Bible is very concerned about all that. Indeed, that is its great central concern, and it has one great remedy for the problem. According to the Bible the one big thing that matters is that we should be right with God. The Bible is, primarily, a book of great principles. Of course it does come down to details, but its main emphasis is on these central principles. It looks out upon mankind trying to improve itself, and it says, 'Yes, that is all right, but it will avail you nothing because you are ignoring the centre. You are treating the symptoms, but you have forgotten that the trouble is at the source.' So it always brings us back to that source, which is that the most important thing of all is our relationship to God.

To put it another way, all our troubles in life, according to the Bible, are ultimately due to the fact that we are in a wrong relationship to God. That has been the Biblical diagnosis for thousands of years and it is as true now as it has ever been–all our ills and all our unhappiness ultimately come back to the fact that we have wandered from God, that we are not in the right relationship to Him. Indeed, the Bible goes further and says that until we do come back to that true and right relationship, nothing will avail us. We can improve ourselves here and there, but if we are centrally wrong, finally we shall be altogether wrong.

That is the great theme of the Bible from beginning to end, and the ways in which it puts that message are almost endless. You get it in plain, direct, unvarnished teaching, but you also get it in some of the people that it puts before us, and we should thank God for them, these characters and illustrations which we have in the Bible, who are, as it were, living representations of its doctrine and teaching.

Take the saints of the Bible, the so-called heroes of the faith; take people like those who are represented in Hebrews 11. They are but samples, just a few of the great list of names that we have in the Old Testament. There are men and women who were in this world exactly as we are, subject to the same vicissitudes, subject to the same things that tend to happen to us in a world like this, and yet, as you look at them, you have to admit that there was something exceptional and outstanding about them. They were people who seemed to be triumphant in life, and their secret, according to the Bible, was only one thing; it was their relationship to God.

Now these were men and women who were independent of their circumstances, and they were what they were because they were right at the centre with God. They suffered terrible trials, they endured adversity in its extremest form, yet you cannot look at them without seeing that they were people who possessed a calmness, a poise and a hopefulness which nothing could destroy. You see things going wrong all around and about them, and yet you see them going steadily forward. And the reason for this, says the author of Hebrews, was their faith. Faith is being in the right relationship to God, knowing Him. Their secret was that they went on 'as seeing him who is invisible' (Heb 11:27); it was because they were right with God that they were made independent of circumstances and chance and conditions and surroundings.

That is typically representative of the biblical teaching, and the message of the Bible to us is still just that. It is not part of the business of Christian preaching and of the Christian Church just to comment about conditions and circumstances and happenings. It is not part of the preaching of the gospel to try to predict and prophesy what will happen in the future. Many attempt to do that, but it is utterly hopeless. It may cheer us up for the time being to be told that something good is going to happen, but it is the old story and it never leads to anything. Rather, the business of Christian preaching is to tell us that whatever the circumstances may be, whatever may be awaiting us in the future, if we are right with God it will not finally matter, it will not have a devastating effect upon us.

Now that is an all-inclusive challenge; the Bible makes that claim and its whole offer is just that: if we are right at the centre with God we can look to the future and say, 'Come what may, all will be well with my soul.' This message, which it puts to us in so many different ways, places us in this happy position of being more or less independent of circumstances and accidents and chance and environment, anything that may happen. It does not try to improve these particular problems; it puts us right. Its case is that if we are right, then we shall be masters of our circumstances, so it always brings us back to that central and all-important matter.

Here, then, is the thing that primarily counts, that we should be right with God, that we should have fellowship with Him, that we should know Him; so that if God calls us, as He called Abraham, to do something which seems to us at that moment to be shattering, we go forward as seeing Him who is invisible; we do it in faith. Or, like Moses perhaps, we may be presented and confronted by a choice which we cannot quite understand, but we will be in no hesitation, 'choosing rather to suffer affliction with the people of God, than to enjoy the pleasures of sin for a season' (Heb 11:25). That is it! We may be called to do things which come to the natural man in an utterly devastating manner, and yet to us, because we are right with God, we will have an understanding and we will not be afraid.

That is the thing which John deals with in these two verses. This epistle, as we have seen,[2] was probably written about A.D. 85 when John was an old man. The words he uses suggest that he was old: he says, 'my little children,' though he was not addressing little children but adults, members of the Church. But to John they were but little children; some had even come into the faith in his own ministry. At any rate, he had taught them, and now the old man at the end of his life, knowing he has not many more years in this world, sees these people, the young Christian Church, confronted by difficulties and problems and trials and tribulations. What can he say to them? He sees the danger, he knows the frailty of human nature, what is it that matters? So his final bit of advice to them is: 'My little children, these things write I unto you, that ye sin not. And if any man sin, we have an advocate with the Father, Jesus Christ the righteous: and he is the propitiation for our sins: and not for ours only, but also for the sins of the whole world.'

As John looks at those people, and as he looks back across his own life, he sees that there are two main dangers that always confront us–he is writing particularly to Christian people. The first is that of complacency, and the other is the exact opposite, the danger of hopelessness. Or, to put it another way, the danger is compromise on the one hand and depression on the other; and the trouble with most of us is that we tend to oscillate between these two. In certain moods and states we are very complacent; we say we are all right, but in the next moment we are feeling utterly hopeless and full of despair. How difficult it is to maintain an even keel, to keep balance, just to be steady and strong and sure, avoiding these extremes that are always there confronting us. That is John's diagnosis, so he provides something which will cater for that very possibility and he divides his message up into two–command and comfort; exhortation and consolation; objective and promise. And the two parts are: what you and I have to do and what God in His infinite grace is always ready to do for us.

Now these, according to the Bible everywhere, are the two most important things for us in this life and world. They are the two things we must always bear in mind if we are anxious to enjoy true fellowship with God. That is John's advice to these people. 'I am going out of the world,' he says in effect. 'I shall not be with you much longer, and the one thing that matters for you is that you should always be walking with God, that you should always be maintaining that fellowship. If that is right, it does not matter very much what will happen to you.'

How, then, is that to be maintained? This is John's reply. First of all there is the word, the command, the exhortation, the objective which we should never lose sight of, but which we should always keep steadily before us: 'These things write I unto you, that ye sin not.' If you want to know God and maintain fellowship with God, do not sin. We shall look later at these two verses in a more purely doctrinal manner, so we shall consider them here in a purely practical sense, and I want to put it as simply as I can. There is very high doctrine in these two verses, doctrine that has often led, and will lead, to a great deal of discussion and disputation, but let us just look at it now quite simply as a practical, direct exhortation.

'That ye sin not.' What does this mean? To answer that, let us ask an apparently almost ridiculously simple question: What is sin? Why should we not sin? Well, sin means that we disobey God's holy law which He has revealed to us. Sin is anything that is condemned in the Bible. It does not matter what it is, if the Bible tells us not to do it then we must not do it: 'Thou shalt not kill'; 'thou shalt not steal'; 'thou shalt not commit adultery.' I feel at times we ought to put the Ten Commandments in the forefront of our preaching. There are certain prohibitions which are absolute and about which there is no discussion, and if you are in a condition of querying and questioning and breaking them, then you will never know fellowship with God; these are absolute where God is concerned. Sin is disobedience to God's revealed law.

It also means disobeying conscience. There is within us all that inward monitor; we have no excuse; before we did that thing we knew it was wrong; there was this voice that told us not to do it, that called us to stop and think. It said, 'No, you cannot do that.' It was there and we knew it was wrong and yet we did it. To disobey conscience is to commit sin. The Bible does not only say that if we are doubtful about a thing we must not do it; it says, 'Abstain from all appearance of evil' (1 Thess 5:22); anything that looks evil, do not do it.

Or, to put it still more generally, sin means that our lives are governed by desires and not by truth. Is this not the very essence of the whole moral psychological problem at the present time? People today are not interested in truth; they say they are entitled to do what they want to do, and if you begin to reason with them they say, 'Why not?'–that is the question–or 'I couldn't care less!' That is the terrible and awful statement that sums it up–this modern spirit of lawlessness, governed by desire, by impulse, by passion and lust and not by standards of truth, not by a clear indication of that which is right and wrong.

We can sum it up like this: to live a life of sin means that we are not governed by God, that thoughts of God are not at the centre of our lives, that we do not ask ourselves, 'What would God have me to do, what does God prohibit?' It means that we are governed by what John, in this self-same chapter, goes on to call 'the world'–the way of the world, the whole attitude of the world. It is that sort of life in which thoughts of God do not come in except perhaps occasionally when men and women are frightened because they have been taken ill or there is a death. It means God has not governed and controlled their lives, that they have been dictated by everything that is apart from God. That is sin, to live and to dwell in that kind of atmosphere and to be living that sort of life; as if God did not exist and as if this were the only world and as if man were the supreme being in the whole universe. That is the negative way of looking at it.

The positive way to view this is, of course, that we live as people who are walking in the light. We must not be content with looking at this question of sin negatively; the best way of not sinning is positively to be living the godly life, and that means walking in the light. In other words, it means living as to God and to His glory.

As the first question in the Shorter Catechism of the Westminster Confession puts it, 'The chief end of man is to glorify God and to enjoy Him for ever.' That is the way to avoid sinning, to start out with this main objective, that I am here to live to the glory of God, that my supreme purpose should be to honour Him and to live in accordance with His holy will. I should ask myself, not 'What do I want?' but 'What does the Lord want? What is the Lord's will? What has He revealed concerning Himself and His purpose?' I start with the great desire to live to His glory, and if I do that I shall not sin.

That, then, is the first way of looking at it; that is what is meant by saying 'that we sin not.' But let me go on to ask a still more practical question–why must we not sin? Let me give you some answers to that question–and I suggest to you that the more we reason these things out, the better it will be for us and the more we shall be unable to sin. Firstly, sin is something which is condemned and hated by God, something which is utterly opposed to Him and His divine and holy nature. That really ought to be enough for us. There is no need to argue about this. I must not sin because God has said I must not; it is abhorrent to Him.

Another reason why I should not sin is that sin is wrong in and of itself and in its own nature. Is this not one of the greatest troubles in life, that we will not look upon these things objectively? Of course we do not do that because we are involved in the process and we are always out to excuse ourselves and to explain away what we have done. But it is important that we should look upon sin objectively, look at its ugliness and its foulness; look at all the misery and wretchedness it produces, look at all the havoc that it makes. If only we could see the real nature of sin, we should hate it, so it behooves us to look at it and examine it. It must be avoided because of its ugliness and because of its twisted and perverted character.

Let me put a still stronger reason to all Christian people. I should not sin because sin is the terrible and foul thing that caused such suffering to my blessed Lord; the thing that brought the Son of God from heaven to earth, in a sense, was just this. The thing that made Him humble Himself and make Himself of no reputation was ultimately the problem of sin. It was sin that made Him endure the contradiction of sinners against Himself; it was the problem of sin that caused Him to sweat drops of blood in the garden of Gethsemane; it was sin that drove the nails into His holy hands and feet; it was sin that produced the agony and the suffering and the shame of the cross–that is what sin does. Can I, as a Christian, go on sinning? 'These things write I unto you, that ye sin not.' You should not desire that which caused Him so much suffering and so much pain.

But let me give you another reason. Sin is dishonouring to the gospel, to its claims and to its power. Here is a gospel which tells us it can give us power; a gospel that offers us life and renewal of strength. So, then, if we sin, we are denying the gospel and bringing it into disrepute, so we must not sin.

Now I put it like this because that is the way in which the New Testament presents its whole doctrine of holiness and the way in which it calls us not to sin. In other words, we are not to be spending our life trying to surrender ourselves, trying to yield ourselves up, trying to let go that God may give us the victory. No! We have to reason it out; we must say, 'I must not sin because God condemns it, because it is wrong in itself, because it caused Christ's suffering, because it is dishonouring to the gospel.' Reason it out–that is the New Testament appeal. 'I write these things unto you, that ye sin not,' and you must know why.

John is concerned fundamentally about our walk with God and our fellowship with Him, and therefore he says, 'My little children, I write these things unto you because sin always ultimately breaks fellowship with God, and therefore immediately casts us off from the source of all our blessedness. It is no use your saying you want to walk with God and then deliberately sinning. The moment you sin, fellowship is broken; the moment you fall into this kind of transgression, you interrupt the fellowship. The one thing that matters is fellowship with God. I do not know what may await you; you may be tried, you may be persecuted, there may be war and calamity, there may be terrible things awaiting you; the one thing that matters is that you are right with God. That being so, do not sin because sin breaks the fellowship.'

Not only that; sin is utterly inconsistent with our profession. It is totally inconsistent with our professed hatred of sin and with our professed desire to be delivered from it. Christians are people who realise and know that sin is the central problem in life and they therefore say that they want to be delivered and emancipated from it. So if they continue to sin, they deny what they profess to believe. Such a position is completely inconsistent and self-contradictory.

And sin also leads always to an evil conscience. When men and women sin, they are under a sense of condemnation, they are unhappy–I am speaking true to experience, am I not? Look back across the past days. When you did something you should not have done, did you not become miserable with yourself and irritable with everybody? Well, it was because you were unhappy; you knew you were wrong and yet you did it, and there you were, miserable and unhappy. 'Little children, these things write I unto you, that ye sin not.' It will rob you of happiness and joy and will give you a sense of condemnation.

But it will even do worse than that, it will lead to doubts; it will, at times, make you feel uncertain of your relationship to God. But still more important is this: it will make you feel you have no right to pray. Have you not experienced that? You do something that you should not do and you get this sense of condemnation; then something happens and you feel you need strength from God and you say, 'I will pray about it.' And then the thought comes to you that you have no right to pray, you have sinned against God, you are a cad to rush to Him just when you want Him; and when everything goes well you do not want Him and you forget Him–have you not found this interruption to prayer? That is why John tells these people not to sin.

It is so practical. It works like this. When we face the future, we wonder what is going to happen; there are so many things that may happen to any one of us–a terrible illness, loss of money, the illness of a dear one, death, war–who knows? Well, these things may happen; we may be utterly helpless. We see that the world cannot help us with all its wealth, its education and its knowledge. We are left there face to face with one of these trials and crises of life. We say, 'I wonder, what of God?' and we are about to pray and then comes this sense of condemnation and somehow we feel we have no right to approach Him. That is why we must not sin. If we want to enjoy fellowship with Him, if we want to be able to pray in the hour of crisis, we must keep the line of communication clear, keep the pathway open, avoid these obstacles that hinder access to God.

And then, lastly, let me put it like this. Sin always leads ultimately to a sense of utter hopelessness, and that is why these New Testament epistles are written. People in that state and condition may sometimes sin for so long that they feel they can do nothing and they have this sense of devastation and of being forsaken.

Those are some of the reasons why we should not sin–that is the command which the Apostle gives to these people.

But let us finish with just a word about the other side: the comfort and the consolation. Thank God there is this further word: 'And if any man sin'–or has sinned–'we have an advocate with the Father, Jesus Christ the righteous: and he is the propitiation for our sins; and not for ours only, but also for the sins of the whole world.' If, therefore, you see as you look back nothing but sins against God, I assure you that if you believe on the Lord Jesus Christ those sins are forgiven you, they are blotted out. 'Ah, yes,' says someone, 'but you do not know how terribly I have sinned, how much I have sinned.' My dear friend, 'He is the propitiation for . . . the sins of the whole world,' and you and all your sins are included. Do not let the devil therefore depress you, do not let him drive you from that optimistic blessing to despair and hopelessness. If you see your sins, as John has already told these people, you have but to confess your sins, and if you do so, 'He is faithful and just to forgive us our sins and to cleanse us from all unrighteousness' (1:9). For the provision is already made, the propitiation has already been provided. He, the Christ, the Son of God, has once and for ever covered all your past sins, all your present sins, all the sins you may commit; the sins of the whole world are covered; the offering has been made once and for ever.

Very well, it seems to me there is only one thing that matters and that can be put in the very little word, 'we.' 'My little children, these things write I unto you, that ye sin not, and if any man sin *we* have an advocate with the Father.' Who are 'we'? Is that the whole world? No, that is not the whole world; that is Christian people, we who know Him, we who have fellowship with the Father, the people to whom he writes, the Christian members of the Christian Church. That is, therefore, the one thing that matters and that counts. Do we know God? Have we fellowship with the Father and with His Son, Jesus Christ? Do I know for certain that Christ is my advocate? I may see myself in six months hence in a terrible predicament. I may want to pray to God and then comes this condemnation of sin and I feel I cannot; and the one thing that will matter then will be that I shall be able to go on and to say, 'I have an Advocate and I can turn to Him; and because of His advocacy I shall know that I am in fellowship with the Father, and God will smile upon me and will grant me His blessing.'

That is the thing that matters in life, that we know Him, Jesus Christ, the righteous one, the advocate with the Father, the propitiation for our sins. Do we know Him? If we do, we know God; and if He is our advocate and representative, our continued fellowship with God is certain and assured.

Thanks be unto God for the heavenly advocate who maintains us in fellowship by His life, by the offering He made once and for ever, and by the power and the life He gives us through the Holy Spirit.

## 2

# Doctrine and Life

> My little children, these things write I unto you, that ye sin not. And if any man sin, we have an advocate with the Father, Jesus Christ the righteous: and he is the propitiation for our sins: and not for ours only, but also for the sins of the whole world.
>
> 1 JOHN 2:1-2

We have considered these verses in general, and, as we have said, in addition to the very practical and essential exhortation, there is also to be found in them a great wealth of doctrine. So we must now look at the doctrinal statements which we find in this mighty statement. This is something which must engage our attention not only because it is always important to consider doctrine, but also because these two verses have so frequently played a prominent part in many discussions and disputes–not to say quarrels–within the Christian Church herself. All those who have any real love for and interest in Christian doctrine must have known how often various statements found in these verses have been the main bone of contention in particular debates and how frequently they are found to be at the very centre of theological dispute and discussion.

So as we come to consider them, it seems to me that nothing is more important than the spirit in which we do so, or, in other words, nothing is so important as our approach to such theological considerations. There are two main dangers with regard to the approach to the doctrinal teaching of the New Testament. The first is the position of those people who say, 'We know that in the past Christian people have spent a lot of their time in discussing doctrine. Our fathers and grandfathers especially were great experts at this. They read books on theology in a way in which people do not do so today. You could not enter into the house of the average Christian without finding certain works on theology; they were always discussing them and arguing about them; they were very interested in theology and doctrine. But,' they say, 'it was often at the expense of more important things.'

So the tendency today is for large numbers to say not only that they are uninterested in doctrine, but also that doctrine is really quite unnecessary. Theological formulae and truth, they maintain, may be of great interest to those who take up that kind of study or to those who have the inclination and time to spend; but what really matters is experience and the kind of life that people live. 'We are not interested,' they say, 'in your various ideas and schools of thought with regard to the precise explanation of how the atonement of Christ works. These things are of no concern to us. So long as we can say "Whereas I was blind now I see," so long as we are living a good life and producing good works, that is the only thing that matters.'

Now what are we to say about that attitude? Well, the reply which I would suggest is appropriate to such people is something like this: 'Whether you like it or not, to speak like that is, in and of itself, to speak in a doctrinal manner. To make statements along that line is, in actual practice, to commit yourself to a particular doctrine. The doctrine of such people is the doctrine of works and, in a sense, of justification by works.' 'Ah, but,' they reply, 'we are not interested in such a term as "justification by works."' But whether they are interested in such terminology or not, that is exactly what they are saying. In other words, you cannot speak about Christianity and religion without being doctrinal. You may reduce the whole of Christian doctrine to just one term, but it is your doctrine all the same.

In other words, whether we like it or not, we cannot avoid doctrine. And we can say the same about religion as we can about doctrine. There is no such thing as an irreligious person; everyone has his or her religion, if you mean by religion that ultimate philosophy or view of life by which people live. Now there are many who say that they do not believe in religion. But not to believe in religion *is* their religion! You cannot speak about these things without automatically and inevitably committing yourself to some particular doctrine or teaching. So there is no way of avoiding the consideration of doctrine; you must be prepared to consider it whether your doctrine is true or false.

But another reason why such people are altogether wrong is that the New Testament everywhere is full of doctrine. So to refuse to consider doctrine is not only to refuse to believe in the Bible as the Word of God, it is insulting to God Himself. If God has chosen to use such terms as righteousness, justification, sanctification, redemption, atonement, reconciliation, propitiation, then it is our duty to face those terms and to consider their meaning; it is dishonouring to God not to do so. Someone may say, for instance, 'I am not interested in all those terms; I believe in God, and I believe in living as good a life as I can in order to please Him.' But how can you please God if you refuse to consider the very terms that He Himself has revealed to the men who wrote the record? This is God's truth, and God has chosen to give us this truth in this particular form, so I must face these terms. My sense of obedience to God compels me to discover as far as I can what He means by them.

Then my third and last reply to such people would be this: The New Testament is never tired of pointing out that to attempt to divorce conduct from belief is always fatal. The Apostle Paul put that in a memorable verse in writing to the church at Corinth when he said, 'Evil communications corrupt good manners' (1 Cor 15:33). He was dealing there with the doctrine of the resurrection, and he said in effect, 'It is no use your saying, "We are not interested in doctrine; we are concerned about life"; if your doctrine is wrong, your life will be wrong.' And that has surely been the tragedy of the last hundred years or so.

That is the danger on the one hand, but there is also a danger at the other extreme which is equally important, and that is the danger which confronts those who have a very great interest in doctrine. So let me try to paint this type of person as clearly as I have painted the other. There are people who are very concerned about doctrine and theology, but their interest seems to be purely detached, purely theoretical and intellectual. There is nothing they delight in more than arguing about theology; yet they do so the whole time as if they were arguing about some abstract science, something far removed from life, something quite apart from practical living. Very often, of course, they do this in what we may describe as a 'party spirit.' In other words, as they read the New Testament they are not as concerned about arriving at a knowledge of truth as they are about discovering arguments to support their own particular theory or idea.

Now it is at that point that we agree to an extent with the criticism of the modern man against many who lived in the past. Let me be perfectly frank and admit that there is a good deal to be said along that line. Far too often our fathers argued about theology and doctrine, and discussed it and preached it in that detached and theoretical way; indeed oftentimes they lost their tempers, forgetting that by so doing they were denying the very doctrine which they claimed to believe.

So this again is a very real danger, and our tendency is always to be swinging from one of these extremes to the other–either no interest in doctrine or the wrong interest in it. Some of us may have to confess to having wasted precious hours of our life, even perhaps days, in a purely intellectual and theoretical interest in doctrinal truths. There is a certain type of mentality to whom nothing is more fascinating than a theological discussion. Indeed, there is a very good case for the argument that there is certainly no higher intellectual work in which we can ever engage. Theology used to be regarded as 'the queen of the sciences.' If you look back across the history of the Church, and indeed secular history, you will find from the bare standpoint of intellectual interest that there has been nothing that has so stimulated man to effort as a consideration of these particular truths.

But therein lies the danger. Our object always should be the discovery of truth, and to expound and understand the Scriptures. We must always compare Scripture with Scripture; and in arriving at an interpretation of particular texts we must always avoid anything which is going to put us in the position of contradicting some other statement of Scripture. Yet we must strenuously avoid the tendency to come to Scripture merely in search of texts to prove our own particular theories and ideas. Doctrine must never be considered in and of itself. Scripture must never be divorced from life.

I say all this by way of introduction because I want to remind you now of some of the doctrines which people have claimed that they have found in these two particular verses. And as I mention them to you, I think you will agree with me that what I have been trying to show about the place of doctrine in the life of the Christian is really of the greatest importance. Here is a question, for instance, that has often occupied the attention of Christian people–the whole question of our activity in the Christian life. Does the Christian have to live an active life in this question of sanctification, or is it just a matter of 'letting go and letting God'? Do we believe in passivity, in a doctrine just of relaxation and of doing nothing, believing that the Holy Spirit is going to do everything? Or do we believe in a kind of activism?

Here, you see, is a statement which has often led to that discussion–'My little children, these things write I unto you, that ye sin not.' There are some people who cannot face a text like that without immediately raising that theological question with regard to activity or passivity. So how do we approach that matter? Well, it seems to me that the most important point is that we should always bear in mind what is clearly revealed by the context of any particular statement, because the danger always is to take a statement out of its context. Our first business always is to try to see what the author is trying to show at this point. What was he concerned about? And if you approach this statement in that way, surely you must come to the conclusion that the Apostle here is not telling these people that if they just do nothing and surrender themselves, then the Lord Jesus Christ will see that they do not sin.

No, what he says is this: 'I am appealing to you not to sin'; it is a command, an exhortation and, of course, we find that it is perfectly in accord with what we find throughout the Scriptures–'put off . . . the old man . . . put on the new man' (Eph 4:22, 24); it is something I have to do. 'Work out your own salvation with fear and trembling' (Phil 2:12); I have to do that. God works in me, but having worked in me, now He asks me to 'work out.' 'Mortify, therefore, your members which are upon the earth' (Col 3:5); not just abandon yourself, surrender yourself, become utterly passive and He will, as it were, cleanse your mind and your subconscious of every sin and evil desire. On the contrary, I have to *mortify* my members; I am exhorted to '*fight* the good fight of faith' (1 Tim 6:12); I am told to '*lay hold* on eternal life' (1 Tim 6:12) and to *flee* from certain sins. I am told to '*reckon*' myself 'to be dead unto sin' (Rom 6:11), and so on.

So there, you see, is one of the statements which we find in these two verses which at once raises the question that has often been a subject for discussion. Now the danger is that as we read a verse like that we could immediately be brought into a great debate as between activity and passivity, and as we do so we could be concerned solely with defining our theory; and thereby both parties would be failing to do the very thing for which the Apostle is appealing. No, the thing about which I should be concerned is not my theory with regard to these matters, but that I should not sin.

Then let me come to a second issue which is perhaps still more important and difficult. Do these two verses teach that the Christian must of necessity sin? 'My little children, these things write I unto you, that ye sin not. And if any man sin, we have an advocate with the Father, Jesus Christ the righteous: and he is the propitiation for our sins.' Is sin inevitable? Must the Christian go on sinning in this life and world, or is a state of perfection possible here and now?

How easy it is to argue about that, and how often have these two verses been used as the base from which such a debate has started. I am sure most Christians have, at some time or another, been engaged in this discussion. Is perfection possible, or is it not? This has been debated throughout the centuries, especially since the teaching of John Wesley with regard to perfection about the middle of the eighteenth century. Here again is one of the dangers that confronts us. We come across these words. Do they mean of necessity that we are liable to sin? And immediately we are in the heart of this great dispute. Often, as this matter is discussed, both parties to the discussion are certainly proving that sin is possible whether it is inevitable or not, by forgetting the real purpose of the Scripture and by being concerned about their particular point of view and defending it at all costs.

Of course, it is an extremely difficult matter; take these words: '*And if.*' What exactly do they mean? One commentator for instance, has written, 'This conditional particle "if" must be regarded as causal, which means this, that we sin.' And that, incidentally, was the exposition of these verses by John Calvin; he said this means that we must sin. He says that the Apostle would not add this immediately–'If you do sin, we have an advocate'–unless he knew for certain that we are open to sin. It is causal, and there you get this one side of this whole debate. And there are those on the other side who would immediately retort that that is dishonouring to the Lord, because He could maintain us in a state of sinless perfection.

So what do we do about this difficulty? It would be utter folly on my part if I were to enter into that discussion as such. Indeed, there is a sense in which I refuse to enter into it, but my reply would be something like this: Our business, surely, is to take the statements of Scripture as they are. All I know is that I am told two things: I am commanded not to sin, but I am given a blessed and glorious assurance that if I do sin, my sin is still covered by the blood of Jesus Christ.

I suggest that this whole discussion with regard to the question of perfectionism is purely theoretical and that in a sense we have no right to sit in our armchairs and argue whether we are perfect or not. Our business is to be striving after perfection, not to sin, and to mortify our members and exert ourselves with all our might to live a life that shall be free from sin. I think the history of the past shows very clearly that if we but theoretically discuss and consider this question of sinless perfection, we shall almost certainly find ourselves falling into sin and at any rate giving practical demonstration that, whether sin is inevitable or not, it is certainly possible, and that it is extremely difficult not to sin. We must hold these two things together: at the same time: 'sin not,' and yet 'if any man sin . . .' As Paul says, 'Let a man examine himself' (1 Cor 11:28); let us face ourselves in the light of this word. When we come to the conclusion that we are sinless and perfect by comparing ourselves with some sinner in the gutters of life, let us examine our thoughts and imaginations, let us look at this word and search it. Let us look at the Lord Jesus Christ Himself, and if we discover that we still have the elements of sin within us and that we are still sinful, let us then immediately face it as we are exhorted to do. Let us not view the whole thing in an abstract, theoretical and detached manner.

There, then, is the second question that has often been raised about these two verses; now let me mention still another.

Some people read these two verses and immediately say something like this: 'Are these two verses not inciting us to sin? Was John not doing something very dangerous when he said these words? Doesn't this lead inevitably to what is called *antinomianism*? Doesn't it tend to make a person say, "Well, it doesn't matter what you do. If you do sin, just confess it and apply the blood of Jesus Christ to your sin and you are forgiven, and all is well." Doesn't this therefore inevitably lead to loose living?'

Now there have, it is true, been people who have misinterpreted this statement, and it has often led quite definitely to antinomianism. Yet it seems to me that anyone who looks at it in this way is denying the whole doctrine which John has set out to teach. If I am prepared to excuse my sin because of this blessed doctrine of the atonement, then I am making merchandise of the cross of Christ, I am putting Him to open shame, and I am trading on Calvary. It is a temptation and a very real one, especially to evangelical people– the temptation comes; you hesitate, then a voice says, 'Well, if you do sin, it will be all right; you will be forgiven.' There are people who thus trade upon the cross and the truth.

All that, according to John, is just because they have never really understood the cross. Why did Christ go to the cross? Was it merely to allow us to go on sinning? Was it merely to enable us to sin lightly and loosely and then confess and be forgiven? No. According to the teaching of the New Testament everywhere it was this: He died on the cross that He might separate unto Himself a 'peculiar people, zealous of good works' (Tit 2:14). The whole purpose of the cross is to deliver us from sin, to rid us from it, to put us in such a standing with God that we can receive this new and eternal life which will enable us to overcome sin and to follow in the steps of our Lord and Master Himself. But, you see, if you take this theoretical teaching and doctrine of theology only, you will be in grave danger of falling into the sin of antinomianism.

Then, finally, there is another danger. Do these two verses teach the doctrine of *universalism* or not? What do we mean by that? 'If any man sin,' says John, 'we have an advocate with the Father, Jesus Christ the righteous: and he is the propitiation for our sins: and not for ours only, but also for the sins of the whole world.' Immediately we are involved in a great theological question: did Christ die only for the elect or did He die for all? Is salvation universal or is it only for some? Has Christ died for all; will all be saved? Will even Satan himself be saved? Propitiation has been made for the sins of the whole world; therefore all must be saved. There is no such thing as an ultimately lost person; all will finally arrive in glory, even the sinners.

Now those are the questions, but what does our text say? This is what we face: 'He is the propitiation not only for our sin but also for the sins of the whole world.' But some people leave out the first person. Surely the verses say something like this. It is a clear statement to the effect that the death of Jesus Christ upon the cross is sufficient propitiation for the sins of the whole world. There is no question about that; and, of course, this is of necessity true, because of His perfect nature, because of His perfect work, His atonement. His work upon the cross is sufficient for the sins of the whole world. That is beyond dispute; it is plainly stated. But that does not mean or imply that when He went to the cross He was going to die for all. What it says is that His death was *sufficient* for all.

Let me put it like this: Do you notice the distinction that is made between two groups of people in this statement? 'My little children'–he is not writing to the world, he is writing to Christian people–'if any man sin, we have an advocate with the Father.' He does not say that the whole world has an advocate with the Father. '*We* have an advocate with the Father, Jesus Christ the righteous: and he is the propitiation for *our* sins.' Then comes the further statement, 'and not for ours only, but also for the sins of the whole world.'

You see the distinction? We are not told here that the Lord Jesus Christ is advocating before God on behalf of the whole world. No, *we* have an advocate with the Father, and the 'we' here refers to the people to whom he was writing–the Christian people who have fellowship with the Apostle, the people who have fellowship with God and with His Son, Jesus Christ. So Jesus Christ, he tells us, is only an advocate for such people. At the same time he says that His work upon the cross was so great and perfect that it is actually a propitiation sufficient for the whole world, though efficient only for those who are Christians, for those who are partakers of this fellowship with the Apostle and with God and with His Son, Jesus Christ.

As you interpret it like that you find, of course, at once that you are consistent with the teaching of the Scriptures everywhere. The Bible always divides this world of mankind into two groups: the saved and the lost; the Christians and the non-Christians; those who are going to glory and those who are going to perdition; the sheep and the goats; the wise virgins and the foolish virgins; the good steward and the bad steward.

The whole world of mankind is divided into these two ultimate groups, so that before I begin to say, 'He died for all, therefore all must be saved and all are going to be redeemed,' let me not only face these two verses which in and of themselves divide mankind up into two groups, but let me likewise see that there they bring us into line with the whole teaching of the Word of God from beginning to end, where the redeemed and the lost are eternally separated and divided.

We have, then, glanced at some of the doctrinal issues which are of necessity raised as we read these two verses together. Now my exhortation, to put it in a final word, is this: Let us, Christian people, not waste our time in mere theoretical, intellectual discussions about activity and passivity. We must consider them, but let us not stop at discussion; let us not just end by talking about sinless perfection; let us not just fall into the sin of antinomianism, or debate or wrangle about universalism. Let us rather listen to the plain words of the Apostle himself. 'Sin not' and 'If any man sin, we have an advocate with the Father, Jesus Christ the righteous.' That is the thing on which we must concentrate. I am called not to sin, but thank God I am assured that, should I sin, the blood of Jesus Christ His Son still cleanses me from the guilt of that sin and will deliver me from all unrighteousness. Let us hold on to doctrine, but let us beware of the terrible danger of a mere theoretical position divorced from life.

# 3

# The Advocate

> My little children, these things write I unto you, that ye sin not. And if any man sin, we have an advocate with the Father, Jesus Christ the righteous: and he is the propitiation for our sins: and not for ours only, but also for the sins of the whole world.
>
> 1 JOHN 2:1-2

We return again to these verses because I am anxious that we should do with them what I am quite sure the Apostle originally intended. In the first chapter we saw:[1] the Apostle was laying down some of the basic principles with regard to this whole question of fellowship with God. That was the great thing, that was the thrilling message that he had to pass on to the people. There he was, an old man, knowing that his end was at hand and he was leaving a number of Christian people, many of them very young. So he was anxious to help them in this wondrous fact of communion with God; he wanted them to know exactly how that fellowship is to be arrived at and how it is to be maintained, and he began by laying down principles.

Here, in a sense, he sums it all up, because he is so afraid of being misunderstood. We are all in grave danger of misunderstanding these things; we will clutch at anything to excuse ourselves or to excuse sin. So he has pointed out two things in the first chapter: that 'God is light, and in him is no darkness at all,' and therefore we must walk with Him in the light. Then, secondly, knowing that to be told this makes us feel hopeless, especially when we fall into sin and feel we have no right to go back to God, he has given us this consolation: 'the blood of Jesus Christ his Son cleanseth us from all sin,' and he has gone on repeating this.

So here, summing it all up he says, 'My little children, these things write I unto you, that ye sin not'–do not take advantage of the consolation; do not say, 'Well, because the blood of Jesus Christ cleanses me from all sin, I need not be particular or careful.' No, I am writing to you, not to encourage you in sin and licence, said the Apostle, but in order to keep you from sinning. Yet again, he could not leave it at that. He was the great Apostle; he had written so much about love, and he loved these Christians–the relationship between them was particularly close and tender and affectionate.

So he goes on: 'And if any man sin . . .'–this is a word to those Christian people who are conscious of sin and failure. If there are those who say they are perfect, well, they need not listen to this; it is a word to those who are conscious of sin and failure and who are aware of their own unworthiness. And it is, I venture to say, perhaps the classic statement of this matter. There is nothing certainly which is more beautiful that has ever been written about it. How is my fellowship to be restored with God when I sin? How can I be forgiven? This is the situation which is envisaged here by the Apostle.

We all, surely, know something about this. The devil is constantly present, he is the adversary of our souls, and if we find ourselves having sinned, he comes to us and whispers, 'You have no right to go back to God! You have been walking in the light and you have fallen into sin. Isn't that sinning against the law? How can God forgive you?' Is that not how he speaks to us? And he has spoken to some people like that for long years. He has kept them in a state of utter wretchedness and misery. They wonder if they have ever been a Christian, and they fail to see how they can be restored to that fellowship with God from which they have fallen because of sin. Now here is the great word to such people; it is a wonderful statement on the doctrine of forgiveness, and it is especially about the forgiveness of the sins of Christian people.

The first great principle is that there is no forgiveness except in the Lord Jesus Christ and through Him. So many people seem to think that God could forgive us our sins without the Lord Jesus Christ, and that is why, of course, they never see the necessity for the Lord Jesus Christ. They say that God is love and God can forgive sin, so if we should fall into sin, all we have to do is to ask God to forgive us and He does so at once. And it is because so many believe something like that, that they never believe on the Lord Jesus Christ, because they have never seen how essential He is. But, you notice, that is the introduction to the whole of New Testament doctrine. The moment sin is mentioned in the New Testament, immediately *He* is mentioned. So I put it like that as doctrine: there is no forgiveness of sin apart from the Lord Jesus Christ. John puts it like this: 'If any man sin'–well, what happens, do we just ask God to forgive us? Not at all! 'We have an advocate with the Father, Jesus Christ the righteous.' Immediately He comes in.

And that, in a sense, is the doctrine of the whole of the Bible; everything in the Old Testament looks forward to this person. Take all that you can read in books like Exodus, Leviticus and Numbers, and in other books, about what God told the nation of Israel in that old dispensation–burnt offerings, peace offerings and various meal offerings and all these things. Go through all the great ceremonials and rituals and everything that was connected with the Tabernacle and the Temple, all these minute instructions–they were all but types and shadows of that which was to happen fully and finally in the Lord Jesus Christ. They did not really deal with sin; they were merely a covering for it for the time being. They were all looking forward, suggestions of that which was eventually to take place. Indeed, God gave all these regulations to the ancient people just to impress upon them this great truth, that He cannot forgive sin by just forgiving it.

That is the object of all that teaching. Something must happen before God can forgive sin. God, because He is holy and righteous, cannot just say, 'Well, you have sinned and I forgive you.' That is the danger, always, of transposing what we do as individuals to what God does. Some argue, 'Surely a parent has the right to forgive a child if the child does wrong and then comes and says it is sorry. So if we can do that, why cannot God do the same? He is infinitely greater and has infinitely greater love.' But the fallacy there is to forget that none of us is righteous and our ideas of righteousness are hopeless. God is absolutely holy and just and righteous, and, if I may say it with reverence, God's nature and personality make it impossible for Him to deal with sin in that way. Something has to be done about sin; the shedding of blood is essential, for without the shedding of blood there is no remission of sins (Heb 9:22). All the Old Testament teaches that and points forward to Christ.

Here we have the doctrine, of course, in all its richness and fulness, and when John at this point comes to consider this question of sin and what can be done about it, immediately he has to talk about Christ, and he does so in this particularly impressive and beautiful manner. So let us take a firm hold of this particular doctrine; without the Lord Jesus Christ we can do nothing, from the beginning of the Christian life to the end. The greatest saint dying upon his deathbed needs Him and His atoning work; it is in Him alone that we are rescued, it is in Him alone that we are forgiven. It is He alone and what He has done for us–indeed it is He Himself, as I am going to show you–who covers all our sins and does away with them–forgiveness!

Therefore, once more we ask ourselves that question which we must never cease to ask: 'Is my whole position and all my thinking centred on the Lord Jesus Christ?' The word of John, as it is the word of the New Testament everywhere, is that Christ is the beginning and the end, the start and the finish, the Alpha and the Omega, the all-in-all, and unless we realise always when we go seeking forgiveness that we have no plea but the Lord Jesus Christ, our relationship to Him is essentially false. That is the first postulate.

Now let us consider this statement more in detail. How does Christ thus accomplish or bring to pass our restoration to fellowship with God? John puts it here in these verses in a very beautiful way. He does it, says John, by being our *advocate*. 'If any man sin'– if any of you should happen to fall into sin–then you, we, all of us together, 'have an advocate with the Father, Jesus Christ the righteous.' John uses the same word in his Gospel, in chapter 16 verse

7, where our Lord said that He would send us another *comforter*. So what is an advocate? An advocate is one who represents another; he stands before a court, and he presents the case of someone else; he represents this person and puts forward the pleas. And John tells us that the Lord Jesus Christ is, for all who believe on Him and trust Him, an advocate with the Father.

However, this word merits our closer attention. We must never think of it as if the Lord Jesus Christ were there pleading for us before an unwilling God. You will find that certain hymns do suggest that, and statements have often been made which sound as if God were opposed to us and as if God, who is utter righteousness and absolute perfection, were there insisting on His pound of flesh and insisting upon His right to punish us for our sins. Then they picture the Lord Jesus Christ as pleading desperately and urgently, trying to persuade the Father and at last succeeding in getting Him to change His opinion.

But that is an impossible suggestion, and we must be very careful not to view this idea of advocacy in that way. It is impossible because we are told so plainly and clearly in the Word of God that 'God so loved the world, that he gave his only begotten Son' (John 3:16). It was not that the Son decided to come on His own and then, having done so, is pleading urgently and passionately for our deliverance. No, it was the Father who sent the Son; it was God who 'sent forth his Son, made of a woman, made under the law' (Gal 4:4); 'God was in Christ, reconciling the world unto himself, not imputing their trespasses unto them' (2 Cor 5:19). So as we consider the advocacy, let us get rid of the idea that God is unwilling and that He is one who is not prepared to forgive.

But at the same time we must be very careful not to go to the other extreme and think that what John means by 'advocate' is just that the work of Christ on the cross prevails and continues throughout eternity and is there always in the mind of God, and that therefore, in that sense, Christ and His work are advocates for us. We must not think that, because that makes it something quite passive, and that is an idea we must reject, not only because of this particular text, but also because of those magnificent words in Hebrews 7 where the whole argument is that 'he ever liveth to make intercession' for us (v 25). He is unlike that Levitical priesthood who came and lived and died and then a new person had to be appointed. The whole point about Him, says the author of Hebrews, is that He *lives.* He is without beginning and without end–it is this eternal priesthood–and it is because 'he ever liveth' that He is able to 'save . . . to the uttermost'–and must for ever and ever irrespective of what may happen–those 'that come unto God by him.'

In other words, it does seem to me that once more we are confronted by a conception that baffles our understanding. But of this we can be quite certain: that as the Lord Jesus Christ looked after His disciples and followers while here on earth, as He looked after their interests and did certain things for them, so He is now equally active for us there in Heaven. He is representing His people; He is there looking after us and our interests. We do not understand it; it is not a conflict between Father and Son; but it seems to me that in the economy of the blessed Trinity, the Father has handed this particular work to the Son.

So there we have this great comfort and consolation that the Lord Jesus Christ is our great high priest, which means not only that He has offered Himself, but more than that, He takes our prayers and transmits and transforms them and passes them on to the throne of God. He adds to our feeble unworthy prayers the incense of His own blessed glorious, perfect person; so He represents us in that way.

Now the early fathers were very fond of putting it like this, and I think it is very good: They used to say that the Holy Spirit intercedes within us and Christ is interceding for us. The Holy Spirit is within us, building us up in Christ, teaching us and guiding us and showing us what to do and what not to do. And there the Lord Himself is making intercession for us and on our behalf, representing us always to the Father. It is a glorious and sublime conception. Is there anything that can be more comforting and more consoling than to know that at this very moment, and always, the Lord of Glory is concerned about you, is watching over you and is concerned about your interests and is there representing you? We are frail and we are weak and we fall and fail, but we have an advocate with the Father. Therefore, when you begin to feel, at the suggestion of Satan, that you cannot turn back to God and face Him, remember, beloved friend, you are not alone. I agree with you; I know the sensation but too well, the feeling that I have no right to approach God, but remember that you have an advocate and He is there to represent you.

So let us now consider something about the nature of the advocacy. Every word, every sentence, every particular word is in a sense full of consolation. We have an advocate, says John '*with the Father*.' Now that word *with* is a most important little word; it means face to face with. It does not mean that He now and again enters in and is allowed to represent us, but rather that He is always there. And it means that He is always, as it were, looking into the face of the Father. We have a suggestion here of the great doctrine of the Trinity, the three persons yet one substance. He is face to face with God, not having, as it were, to make an application to God to plead for us to the Father; He is always looking into the eyes of the Father. What a wonderful idea, that the one who represents us is always there in that absolute intimacy with God.

So when you have sinned and are full of a sense of shame and guilt and you feel you have no right to go back to God, remember that God in Christ has become your Father; we have an advocate '*with the Father*,' not a God that is opposed to you, a great force or power, but one who loves you with an infinite Father's love. Is there, I ask you again, any greater consolation possible than that?

Let us next go on to ask a second question: Who is this advocate? Look at the description: 'Jesus Christ the righteous.' John did not write these things accidentally. You remember that in the first chapter he talks about 'the blood of Jesus Christ his Son,' and here he says, 'Jesus Christ the righteous.' The words are carefully chosen, inspired; he is controlled as he writes them. The author of Hebrews also writes, 'We have not an high priest which cannot be touched with the feeling of our infirmities; but was in all points tempted like as we are, yet without sin' (Heb 4:15). You see the comfort and consolation? When you are conscious of guilt, when you are conscious of your smallness and frailty and think of God in His utter holiness in the heavens, when you are tempted to ask how God can understand a human being who falls like this, the answer is, 'You have an advocate who understands you perfectly–Jesus.' Read Hebrews 4 and 5 and you will find it worked out at great length and in a most glorious manner. The very Son of God became Jesus, became man, in order that He might understand us. We have a sympathetic high priest; we have one who knows something of our frailty. He knew the frailty of the body; He was tired; He knew what it was to feel weak; so He knows our infirmities. He understands our ignorance, therefore, because He has been a man amongst men. There He is–the Lord of Glory but still Jesus. He has not forgotten what the life of man is in a difficult world like this. Remember that when you are tempted to despair and when you feel God can never take you back. One is representing you who has a feeling and a sympathy for you, an understanding of you and of your infirmities.

He is *Jesus Christ*–and this means of course that He is the anointed one, the appointed one. Therefore, get rid, once and for ever, of the idea that God is against you. It is God who appointed the Son to this particular task of advocacy; it is God Himself who gave Him the office. The high priest was never self-appointed, argues the writer of the epistle to the Hebrews–he was always called of God (Heb 5:4); and God appointed and set apart and anointed the Son to be the Saviour and the representative of those who believe on Him. So, comfort yourselves with this thought: the advocate has been appointed by the judge. The Father, in His everlasting love, has Himself set His Son apart and anointed Him for this particular task. Come to your advocate, therefore, with confidence and with assurance.

But there is still another word–'*the righteous*.' This is, I think, the most wonderful thing of all, and this is the ground of my assurance. John is referring to Christ's character; though He became man, yet He never sinned. No fault was found in Him. He is absolutely perfect, and I need such a representative in the presence of God because of the holiness and the absolute righteousness and justice of God. No one who is himself unworthy can possibly plead for another. Before I can have confidence in my advocate, I must know that He is accepted of God and can stand in the presence of God. No one else could ever have done that; no one but the Son of God is fit to stand in the presence of God and plead. But He is 'Jesus Christ the righteous'!

Thank God, I can rely upon Him never to plead anything that is wrong or unworthy. We can have absolute confidence in this advocate; He will never put forward a plea unless it is right, and this is the righteousness John speaks of. The Lord Jesus Christ does not merely ask God to overlook our sin or forget it; He stands there, and, if I again may use language with reverence in discussing such a high and holy matter, He is there, as it were, to say to God, 'It is but right and just that You should forgive the sins of these people, for I have borne their sins and the punishment of their sins.' The advocate turns to the Father and says, 'I must ask You to put Your law to the side. I am here just to remind You that the law has been fulfilled, that the death has been died, the punishment has been enacted; they are free because I died for them.' It is He who enables God to be at one and the same time just and the justifier of the ungodly (Rom 3:26). Can you imagine greater comfort and consolation than that? As the result of Jesus Christ and His standing in the presence of God on my behalf, I say this–I say it with trembling and yet I say it with confidence–God would be unjust if He did not forgive my sin. Christ has died for me; it is righteous and just for God to forgive the sins of all who believe on the Lord Jesus Christ–Jesus Christ the righteous!

And lastly, the basis of His advocacy is all put in this one word: '*propitiation*.' To propitiate means to render favourable, to turn one towards another with an eye of favour and of pleasure. And what we are told here is that Jesus Christ Himself is our propitiation; not only what He did, not simply the blood that was shed, but that He Himself is our propitiation. It means that He is the high priest and the offering. In the old dispensation everything the high priest took was outside himself, but Christ is His own offering–He is the sacrifice and the high priest. Therefore, says John, He is not only the propitiating sacrifice, but the propitiation itself; everything that is necessary to reconcile the sinner with God is in Jesus Christ. He is prophet, He is priest, He is king. He is the sacrifice; it is His blood that has been shed and presented, and He has purified the heavenly tabernacle; it is all in Him. We need nothing else, we need no one else; He Himself is the propitiation. And because it is the Son of God who is the propitiation, we need have no fear about our sin. We can say with John that He is enough, sufficient to cover the sins of the whole world. Therefore when Satan, your adversary, comes and tries to drive you to the depth of despair and dejection because you have fallen into sin, turn upon him and say, 'I have an advocate with the Father, Jesus Christ the righteous, and He is the propitiation not only of my sin but of the sins of the whole world. I am accepted by God, the fellowship is restored, and I continue upon my way.'

That is the New Testament doctrine of reconciliation; that is its doctrine of the forgiveness of sins. That is the way, and the only way, whereby any one of us can ever come into fellowship with God or can ever be maintained in that glorious fellowship. 'We have an advocate with the Father, Jesus Christ the righteous.'

# 4

# Knowing That We Know Him

And hereby we do know that we know him, if we keep his commandments. He that saith, I know him, and keepeth not his commandments, is a liar, and the truth is not in him. But whoso keepeth his word, in him verily is the love of God perfected: hereby know we that we are in him. He that saith he abideth in him ought himself also so to walk, even as he walked.

1 JOHN 2:3-6

The Apostle here, at the beginning of the third verse, proceeds to apply the doctrine which he has been laying down from the beginning of his letter. The great theme, we remember, is that of fellowship with God–fellowship with the Father and with His Son, Jesus Christ; that is the great thing which had prompted the Apostle to write at all. We have seen that fellowship with God is only possible in and through the Lord Jesus Christ and His perfect work. And indeed John has shown us so clearly that as we go forward in this walk with God, even should we fall into sin, that does not make our position hopeless. He shows us that even that is dealt with by the atoning work of our Lord as He presents it to the notice of the Father. He is pleading, an advocate presenting a case, and in the light of that we have this great certainty concerning the whole basis of our standing in the presence of God. That is the fundamental doctrine, and it is because it is fundamental that we have spent so much time with it. It is the foundation on which everything else that he is going to say in the letter is to be built; and you can never be too careful about the foundation. That is the part of the work on which you expend unusual care, and, therefore, we have not hurried, in order to make quite sure that we are resting on nothing at all save on Jesus' blood and righteousness, and that it is in Him and in Him alone that we have any hope whatsoever.

So having dealt with that, the Apostle now goes on to state certain other matters which are of great practical importance. The Christian life is a *life*; it is not a matter of intellectual assent to doctrine, and therefore he has to deal with the whole thing in a very practical manner. There are certain things which will interrupt our fellowship with God, and we must be very careful about them. So John, in these verses 3-6, deals with one of these matters, and as we shall emphasise later, it is most important to observe that this is the thing that he puts first.

As he comes to do this, he introduces to us a number of his typical, characteristic words. All these Biblical writers have their favourite words; it is one of the romantic aspects of the whole doctrine of inspiration. Inspiration does not mean mechanical dictation; the personality of these men is here. And as we all have favourite words, as every preacher has words which he tends to repeat, so these men have theirs; Paul had his and so did John and Peter. Well now, John's favourite word appears here, the word *know*–'hereby we know'–and if you read his Gospel and epistles again, you will find that it is there everywhere. He is also very fond of the word *abide*, as we see in John 15, and here it is again–you will find it running through this epistle. Then he also likes to play with the words *keep* and *walking*.

Incidentally, it is a point of interest as you study the problems of authorship–not only the authorship of these epistles, but also that of the Gospels–that these things make it abundantly plain and clear that these men wrote the Gospels as they did the epistles. And it is well to bear that in mind, because it is almost certain that the man who wrote this letter was taking it for granted that the people were already familiar with his Gospel. His primary concern here is not merely to know the gospel but to work it out, as it were, and so he uses the same terminology, and we see this interesting connection between the Gospel and the epistle–the laying down of the doctrine and the working out of the doctrine in life as well.

So we come to more practical matters, and yet we shall still find that it is full of doctrine, again a point which we are never tired of noticing in the New Testament. The New Testament, while in an intellectual sense does divide and separate between doctrine and application, nevertheless never parts them in a radical sense. The application is always the outcome of doctrine; you talk about the source of a river and the river itself; while there is a division, in a sense there is no division. And doctrine is remarkably like that; doctrine and practice and yet both are one in an organic and vital sense.

So let us look at what the Apostle has to say to us, and let us take it in this way. He tells us that the Christian should *know* something; in other words, he introduces the great doctrine of assurance–'hereby we do know that we know.' Now I like that, because it is a perfect way of putting it. Peter tells us, 'make your calling and election sure' (2 Pet 1:10), which is perhaps an equally good way of putting it, but there is something about this verse of John's which surely does fix it once and for ever. Christians are people who know what they know.

I remember once hearing a master describe a pupil, and I think he paid that pupil a very great compliment. He said, 'That boy knows what he knows.' He did not say, 'That boy knows everything,' but that he was certain of the knowledge he possessed; he had mastered it, he had got it. Now that is what John tells us about the Christian; indeed the whole object of his letter, in a sense, is to give an exposition of this doctrine of assurance. You will find he goes on saying that. He says, as he looks back at the very end, in the last chapter, 'These things have I written unto you that believe on the name of the Son of God; that ye may know that ye have eternal life' (5:13).

This, therefore, is a very vital doctrine. Yet for some remarkable reason there are many people who seem to have a rooted objection to it. I find it very curious that anyone who claims the name of Christian should be capable of objecting to the doctrine of assurance, because it is in many ways the most glorious truth of all. As natural human beings we want assurance; we want to be certain of things in this life and world, and one of our greatest difficulties is that we are uncertain about so many things. Yet when the New Testament comes and offers us this blessed assurance, there is something instinctive in us, as a result of sin, that objects to it.

Now there are some reasons for that. There are some who feel it is presumption; they show a kind of mock modesty. They say, 'Who am I to presume to say that I know Him. He is so utterly and absolutely holy, and I am so aware of my own sinfulness and unworthiness, how can I claim this? What right have I to say, "I know whom I have believed," or "I know that my sins are forgiven?"' And there are others, I know, who are antagonistic to the doctrine because of their reaction to certain people who believe it. They say in effect, 'Well, I don't want to be like those people who say they know–those glib, superficial people who talk in terms of positive assurance and who, as they are doing so, seem to deny the very thing they are saying. There is a loudness about them and a self-satisfaction.'

Now let us be perfectly fair. There is a sense in which we can understand people reacting against such an attitude, and that is why we must be so careful that our personality and actions and everything that is true of us should be in conformity with the claims which we make. But while there is a sense in which one can understand the people who are antagonised in that way, it is always a very poor argument to refuse a doctrine simply because of other people. Indeed, I think I can prove that to you quite logically and conclusively. If you are going to judge everything in terms of liking certain people, then you will end by believing nothing. You cannot belong to a political party, or any other party, without finding that there are always people you do not like, and so you will find that you have to come out of everything!

But the final answer is that whatever certain people may do, the New Testament is full of this doctrine; indeed, it is, finally, the only solution that the New Testament offers to people in a world like this. You see, the New Testament's picture of life in this world is a very dark and gloomy one. It talks about 'wars and rumors of wars' (Matt 24:6), and it prepares people for persecution and trials and tribulations. But this is the way to come through it–that we know that we know Him; that we have this blessed assurance that 'neither death, nor life, nor angels, nor principalities, nor powers, nor things present, nor things to come, nor height, nor depth nor any other creature shall be able to separate us from the love of God, which is in Christ Jesus our Lord' (Rom 8:38-39).

That was Paul's comfort and consolation. There he was, an old man, a prisoner at the end of his life. So how did he keep going? 'I know whom I have believed, and am persuaded that he is able to keep that which I have committed unto him against that day' (2 Tim 1:12). The New Testament is full of it, so that apart from anything else, not to believe this doctrine is really to deny one of the most central of the New Testament doctrines.

Here, then, the Apostle John puts it quite plainly to us: what are we to know? And he tells us that there are two main things. Firstly, we are to know the Lord Jesus Christ. Let us be quite clear about this. 'Hereby we do know that we know him'; he does not say we are to know certain things *about* Him. No, rather, he says, we are to know Him. He has just been telling us about Him. He is our 'advocate with the Father, Jesus Christ the righteous'; He is 'the propitiation for our sins: and not for ours only, but also for the sins of the whole world.' And what John says here is that we are to know that we know Him.

There are certain matters which I always feel should truly be put in the form of a question, and this is one. Do we know Him? I am not asking whether we know certain things about Him. We know about His birth as a baby in Bethlehem; we know about Him as a boy in the Temple; we know He was a carpenter; we have read the Gospels; we know about the miracles. We are full of knowledge of these things. But that is not what John has in mind. It is something personal, direct, immediate, this word *know*.

Now the Bible is always very strong. It does not mean a general, superficial acquaintance; there is an intimacy about it, a knowledge in a special sense; it is a *personal* acquaintance, an intimacy and an interest. It is nothing less than that, and John says that we should know the Lord Jesus Christ in that way. Our fellowship is to be with the Father and with His Son; and in this verse the 'Him' is undoubtedly a reference to the Son about whom he has been speaking, but it includes a knowledge of the Father also. So we are back again with this fundamental question, this question which we should really ask ourselves every time we pray: Do I know God? Am I simply going to offer up a prayer of hopes and fears and aspirations, or do I know that God is there; is the Lord Jesus Christ real to me?

That, the New Testament tells us, is the Christian position, not to believe things about Him but to know Him. So let us examine ourselves by this test. Are you able to hold conversations with the Lord Jesus Christ and to have fellowship and communion with Him?

The second thing we are to know, John tells us, is that we are in Him. Let me remind you of our text: 'And hereby we do know that we know him, if we keep his commandments. He that saith, I know him, and keepeth not his commandments, is a liar, and the truth is not in him. But whoso keepeth his word, in him verily is the love of God perfected: hereby know we that we are in him. He that saith he abideth in him ought himself also so to walk, even as he walked.'

Here is the other doctrine which John is constantly teaching, that we are not even to stop at a knowledge of Him in a sense of a personal, intimate acquaintance. We are to be aware of a union with Him, this mystical union of the believer with Christ. It is one of the great New Testament phrases–'in Christ.' In Romans 16, in the list which Paul gives of those to whom he sends his regards, he, referring to certain people, says they were 'in Christ before me.' You can find this everywhere in the New Testament; we are incorporated into Christ, we are in Him in the sense that any one member of my body is in the body–'Ye are the body of Christ,' says Paul, 'and members in particular' (1 Cor 12:27).

So the Christian is in Christ. That analogy which is used in John 15 puts this perfectly, the reference to the branch and the vine. It is a vital, organic relationship–not a mechanical attachment, but a live one; it is sharing the life of the vine itself. And that is the relationship of Christians to their Lord. John tells us we ought to know that we are in that vital, organic relationship; we should know that we are a part of Christ, that we are in Him and He is in us and we have received of His life.

And here we see again the great New Testament doctrine of regeneration. Christians are not just people who hold a number of opinions, though they do hold opinions. They are not only men and women who are aware of forgiveness; they are people who can say, 'I live; yet not I, but Christ liveth in me' (Gal 2:20). They are aware of another quality of life; they are aware of the life of the Son of God Himself in their lives; they are in Christ, and the life of Christ has come into them and through them. Now what John tells us is that we must know these things–'We know that we know.' Do you know that you are in Him in that way? Do you know for certain that His life is in you? This is the great principle which John emphasises.

How does the Christian know these things? That is the second point; or, to put it another way, let us consider the basis of this knowledge. How do we test the validity of our experience? It is a most important subject. There can be very little doubt but that John as he wrote these words had certain people very definitely in his mind. We have already referred, in dealing with the first chapter in my book *Fellowship with God,* to the Gnostics of this early century. There were, you remember, certain people who laid claim to some special knowledge. The mystery religions had already started, these strange amalgams of the Christian faith and eastern religions which were sometimes an admixture of philosophy and mysticism.

Now this is something that was not confined to the ancient world. I think you will find that there are quite a number at the present time. Philosophers tend to become mystics. It is a curious thing; it sounds contradictory at first, and yet in the end it is not contradictory at all. These men of ability and understanding have set out as philosophers, and they claim that by thinking and reasoning, they can discover the whole meaning of life. They set out to do so, and then, after a while, in utter honesty, they have to admit they have not succeeded. So they say, 'What is to be done?' and their tendency is to pass by, as it were, the gospel of Jesus Christ, which is here in the centre, and to swing from philosophy right over to mysticism. Having tried reason, they in a sense abandon it and submit themselves to some strange mystical experience.

There were people like that in the ancient world, and I have no doubt John had this in mind. They had been initiated–that was the word–into some mystic truth. They met together, and there things were revealed to them. They were always talking about their experiences, and they said that they had this unusual knowledge as a result. Read the epistle to the Colossians with that in your mind as a background and you will find it most illuminating.

So John deals with the question in this way. 'It is very important,' he says, 'that you should test your experience; every experience is not a true one, for there are false experiences. So prove the spirits, test them, examine them. Do not believe every spirit; there are antichrists and false spirits. The devil transforms himself into an angel of light. He can counterfeit most of the Christian experiences–I do not say all, but most–so if you have an experience, you must test and examine it. Now,' says John, 'there are people who claim they have an unusual knowledge of Christ and they are claiming a mystic experience, so how do you test it?'

And here he leads us to his great first test. This is of vital importance, because I find in my experience as a minister that there are large numbers of people who are unhappy about themselves and their Christian life simply because they have not had the same unusual experience which somebody else has had. They have not, for example, had the experience of seeing a ball of fire and feeling that the whole room has been illuminated, and because of that they do not feel that they are Christians at all. They say that they have not had this special vision and thereby they are robbed of the wonderful experience that the New Testament has to give.

How may I know that I know Him? Well, observe how John puts it, and I must say there is to me almost an element of divine humour at this point. People are fond of describing John as a mystic. You will find there are certain people who do not like the Apostle Paul, but they like John. They say that Paul argues too much and that there is too much logic and reason about him, whereas John is full of love and mysticism.

So how interesting it is that John, who is described as the mystic, is the man who tells us that the way to test ourselves is not to seek for some mystical experience, but to examine our conduct and our lives! 'Hereby we know that we are in him'; not by the strange, the mystical, far from it; it is as prosaic as this: 'If we keep his commandments'; nothing less than that. It is not experience that enables us to say that we know Him; it is not feelings, not sensations, not visions, not amazing answers to prayer, not thrills, nor the unusual. We are all familiar with this kind of thing. There are so many who seem to think that the only way in which you can be absolutely sure is that you have one of these things and that you should always be talking about them. But no, says John, that is not what comes first, that is not the safe thing.

Now God forbid that anyone should misunderstand me! There *are* experiences in the Christian life, and I thank God for them, rare experiences that come, certain things like those which the Apostle Paul experienced and which he is almost afraid to mention. He says, 'I do not talk of that man taken up into the third heaven some fourteen years ago, but rather thank God that these things are possible' (see 2 Cor 12). However, these are not the things that John puts first. Here is the first test: What is your life like; how do you live? The test whereby we know we are His is this: are you keeping His commandments?

Keeping His commandments does not mean I just put on the wall a list of specific injunctions and do my best to keep them. Rather, it means that I am always concerned to be living the Christian life as fully as I can; that my great object is to be well-pleasing in His sight. I know what He wants me to do; I find it in the Old and in the New Testaments. I have the Ten Commandments and the Sermon on the Mount which apply to me, and I have the whole moral, ethical teaching of the New Testament. Those are His commandments and I have to keep them. 'And if you can say quite honestly,' says John, 'that you are very concerned about doing that; if you can say you are striving to do that and that that is your ambition in life, you can know that you are in Him, for to know Him is to walk as He walked.' 'He that saith he abideth in him ought himself also so to walk, even as he walked.' That puts it perfectly once and for ever.

The Bible often describes our life as a walk. 'Enoch *walked* with God' (Gen 5:24); 'Noah *walked* with God' (Gen 6:9). Then read what God said to Abraham in Genesis 17:1–'*Walk* before me, and be thou perfect.' 'I,' said Jesus Christ, 'am the light of the world: he that followeth me shall not *walk* in darkness, but shall have the light of life' (John 8:12). Then, listen to Paul saying the same kind of thing: 'For ye were sometimes darkness, but now are ye light in the Lord: *walk* as children of light' (Eph 5:8).

It is a wonderful picture of the Christian life; it is a journey; we walk along, and what John says here quite simply and without any explanation is this: 'If you say you are in Him, then you ought to walk as He walked. Look at His walk, look at His demeanour, see how He lived His life in the world. If you say that you are in Him, if you say His life is in your life, if you say you are like the branch to the vine, then you will bear the character of the tree–that is inevitable. That which takes of the life of something represents and manifests that self-same life. If you, therefore, say you are in Him, you ought also to walk as He walked.'

See how our Lord walks through the pages of the four Gospels. The first thing you see is a humble, lowly and meek person. 'A bruised reed shall he not break, and the smoking flax shall he not quench' (Isa 42:3). 'Come unto me . . .,' He says, 'learn of me; for I am meek and lowly in heart' (Matt 11:28-29). It is as we look at Him, as we begin to examine ourselves, that we feel we have no right to be here at all. There is so often a hardness about our testimony; we think we are in Him; we imagine we are testifying to the power of the Christian life. But the great thing we know about Him is that He was meek and lowly. The world does not encourage modesty, and I am afraid that at times the Church today does not do so either. We try to imitate the world, and we become self-assertive. We are so afraid of being called weaklings by the world that we develop into a boisterous kind of Christian. But I do not see that in the New Testament–meek and lowly.

The Corinthians in their folly said of the great Apostle Paul that his presence was 'weak, and his speech contemptible' (2 Cor 10:10), though he was introducing the meekness and the lowliness of his Lord. We are anxious to impress, and it is as true of the Church as it is of the world. The Church would turn the preacher into a man of great and dominating personality. How different that is from what we find here; we ought to walk as Christ walked. His great concern was to do the will of God, to please Him and not to please men. He was a man of sorrows and acquainted with grief. He mourned because of the sin of this world; it hurt, it pained Him. Do we share something of His godly sorrow because of the state of the world? Paul puts it like this in 2 Corinthians 5:4: We 'do groan, being burdened.' Do we groan? Do we give the impression of being burdened because of the sin and iniquity that is rampant around and about us? That is how He walked, and that is how we ought to walk.

And above all we see in Him love to God and love towards men and women–His compassion, His sympathy, His patience, His lovingkindness.

Well, according to the Apostle John, that is the test we are to apply to ourselves. Not the thrills and the visions, but that within me I feel a great desire to be like Him, to follow in His steps, to walk as He walked, to keep His commandments and to fulfil His word.

This is an inevitable test. Now John does not say, 'If you live that life you are making yourself a Christian,' but rather, 'If you are a Christian this is how you live.' If you have the life, it is bound to show itself, and if it does not, then you have not the life. That is logical; it is absolutely inevitable. These things are not matters to be argued about; we just face the facts. You cannot be receiving the life of Christ without becoming like Him. You cannot walk with God without keeping His commandments. You cannot know God without immediately, automatically loving Him. Love always manifests itself by doing what the object of its love desires.

There, then, is the first great test, the safest test; not the strange mystical initiation into some new knowledge, but keeping His commandments, keeping His word, walking even as He walked.

So again, do you know that you know Him? Does your life prove to you that you do? If these are the things you are most concerned about, it is because you know Him. God grant that we all may be able to say together, 'I know that I know Him.'

5

# Loving the Brethren

> Brethren, I write no new commandment unto you, but an old commandment which ye had from the beginning. The old commandment is the word which ye have heard from the beginning. Again, a new commandment I write unto you, which thing is true in him and in you: because the darkness is past, and the true light now shineth. He that saith he is in the light, and hateth his brother, is in darkness even until now. He that loveth his brother abideth in the light, and there is none occasion of stumbling in him. But he that hateth his brother is in darkness, and walketh in darkness, and knoweth not whither he goeth, because that darkness hath blinded his eyes.
>
> 1 JOHN 2:7-11

These five verses must obviously be taken as a whole because they contain one particular, great message. So before we consider them in detail, let us observe first of all the connection between them and what has gone before. John has just said that the final proof any man can have of the fact that he is a Christian is that he keeps, and delights in keeping, and goes on keeping, the commandments of the Lord. There, he says, is something which is really safe as a test, much safer than any experience that one may have had, certainly much safer than any feelings or sensations that one may be conscious of within. Here is an objective test, and yet, obviously, a proof of life itself.

Then, having laid that down, John, as we have been considering, very naturally and almost inevitably brings it down to the realm of the particular. And so he now brings us to this vital and all-important New Testament doctrine of the *love of the brethren.*

Here again we are face to face with something which is absolutely vital to the Christian position. John is concerned about our fellowship with God, so he has been telling us there are certain things that hinder it, and here is another and one of the most important of them. To fail to love the brethren will interrupt our fellowship with the Father and therefore will rob us of many of the blessings of the Christian life.

But we can also put it in a different way, and this is true of every one of these items that John singles out. It also provides us with a very wonderful test of our whole position. You see, we can go on looking at this epistle constantly in a two-fold manner. We can look at the various things that John enumerates as the things that hinder the fellowship, and we can also see them all as tests of our Christian position, and so you will find that when people have studied this epistle, they have generally looked at it from one of those two standpoints. But both are true, and it would be well for us always to bear the two in mind.

John starts off by putting it like this: 'Brethren, I write no new commandment unto you, but an old commandment which ye had from the beginning. The old commandment is the word which ye have heard from the beginning. Again, a new commandment I write unto you, which thing is true in him and in you: because the darkness is past, and the true light now shineth.'

Now, people are sometimes puzzled as to the meaning of this 'old' and 'new,' and the answer is really to be obtained by considering John 13:34 where our Lord Himself used this expression: 'A new commandment I give unto you, That ye love one another. . . .' There is a sense in which this exhortation to love one another, to love the brethren, is at one and the same time old and new.

It is old in this sense: 'I am now going to tell you something you already know,' says John in effect. 'In other words, from the moment you first heard the gospel, you heard this particular doctrine emphasised. I shall not add to the gospel which you have already believed and received. I am simply reminding you of what you already know.' So it is an old commandment, and an essential part of the Christian position. Integral to the gospel of Jesus Christ is the whole conception of a new family with the members loving one another; so in that sense it is not new. You will also find it in the Old Testament. It is there in the Old Testament law: 'Thou shalt love thy neighbour as thyself' (Lev 19:18), so that even when our Lord talked about a new commandment He was in a sense simply emphasising that old commandment that had been given to the children of Israel long ago. They had been separated as God's people, and God had told them that they must have this love one to another.

But though it is in that sense an old commandment, it is also a new one in that it is possible now in a way that it was never possible before. The Lord Jesus Christ, by coming into this world and by doing what He has done, has made this old commandment in a sense a new commandment because there is a new possibility connected with it. John puts it like this: 'Again a new commandment write I unto you, which thing is true in him and in you.' 'This thing,' says John, 'which I am now emphasising has been realised in Him and in you. Look at the people in the old dispensation. They had this command to love, and yet they found it very difficult. But in the Lord Jesus Christ we see it fulfilled and carried out. The Lord Jesus Christ has fulfilled the law of God. He loved men and women in the sense that the Old Testament meant; it has been realised in Him, and it is true in Him.'

'But not only that,' says John, 'it is also realised in you, it is true in you.' In other words, the Lord Jesus Christ has made it possible for us to keep this commandment in an entirely new manner. John is here reminding them that they are left without excuse; it is possible now for Christians, as the result of receiving new life from Christ, as the result of the power of the Holy Spirit, to love their fellow men and women, to love their brethren in the way that God originally intended. As we, as Christians, consider this commandment, there is a sense in which it is absolutely new.

It is idle to ask the world to love the brethren because it is incapable of it, as I am going to show you. That is why it seems to me that it is quite a heresy to approach the world, which does not believe on the Lord Jesus Christ, with the gospel of the New Testament and say, 'Practise that.' That is why it seems to me to be an utter illusion for anyone to think that you have only to preach Christian ethics to the world and then you can banish wars and disturbances, because the world is incapable of it. But to Christians there is a new possibility. They have received a new life; they have the life of Christ in them, and as Christ loved, so Christians can love. But nobody else can, so that in this setting it is a new commandment. It has been realised in Christ and in all who have received life from Him. So having laid down that background, John now goes on to make this appeal, this exhortation to these Christian people, to love one another.

Let me put it to you in the form of some two or three propositions. The first thing we have to see is that Christ has brought into this world a new order of life which has changed everything; the difference that He has made is, in a sense, the difference between light and darkness. Notice again–'because the darkness is past, and the true light now shineth.'

This is, of course, absolutely vital to the whole New Testament position. The Apostle Paul likes to put it in this way: 'Therefore if any man be in Christ, he is a new creature: old things are passed away; behold, all things are become new' (2 Cor 5:17). Or he puts it like this: 'Wherefore know we no man after the flesh: yea, though we have known Christ after the flesh, yet now henceforth know we him no more' (2 Cor 5:16). Being a Christian has changed everything; we are like new people in a new world; nothing is the same as it was before.

And John is saying exactly the same thing here. He has said that this world is a realm of darkness; we have already seen him emphasising that in the first chapter where he talks about 'walking in the light' and 'walking in darkness.' And here he comes back to this same conception. Again the Apostle Paul uses exactly the same language in writing to the church at Colosse; he talks about our being 'delivered . . . from the power of darkness, and . . . translated . . .

into the kingdom of his dear Son' (Col 1:13). The Apostle Peter has the same idea when he says, '. . . which in time past were not a people, but are now the people of God . . . who hath called you out of darkness into his marvellous light' (1 Pet 2:10-9). Indeed the New Testament is full of this. Our Lord Himself said, 'I am the light of the world: he that followeth me shall not walk in darkness, but shall have the light of life' (John 8:12). That is the essential part of the New Testament picture of the Christian and of the Christian position.

But in order to show you fully the way in which the New Testament puts this, we must consider verse 11: 'But he that hateth his brother is in darkness, and walketh in darkness, and knoweth not whither he goeth, because that darkness hath blinded his eyes.' The metaphor is rather involved, but to put it simply, John is saying that people who are not Christians are walking in the dark; yes, but not only that, there is a darkness within them also. The trouble with sinners and unbelievers is not simply that they have darkness around and about them and cannot see where they are going; the darkness has blinded their own eyes–they are blind as well as being in the dark. It is of real and vital importance that we should bear those two concepts in mind. Unbelievers are in the realm of darkness, and they themselves are in a state of darkness, so that, in a sense, even if you put them into the light they would not be able to see. So when people become Christians, two things happen to them: their own eyes are opened, and they are enabled to see; and they are also in an entirely new realm.

Now both these conceptions, as we have seen, are to be found constantly in the New Testament. Those who become Christians are those who are translated from the kingdom of darkness into the kingdom of light, or into the 'kingdom of his dear Son.' Their position has been changed, yes, but they themselves are also changed. The god of this world had blinded their eyes, so that they could not see the gospel; but now their eyes have been opened, they have been enlightened, and let me emphasise again the importance of bearing those two aspects in mind. I am changed, and I am in a new realm; I am a different person, and I am a citizen of a different kingdom. Both things are true. I am not simply the man I was in a new kingdom. I am a new man in a new kingdom, and the two things come out here in the language employed by the Apostle.

So the thing we have to hold on to is that if we are truly Christian people, we are left without an excuse in this matter of brotherly love. The darkness is passing away, the light has come, and we are a new people. There is no excuse for us whatsoever, if we are not fulfilling the commandment.

But, secondly, therefore, whether or not we belong to this new order is proved by our behaviour in the matter of love. The test of whether we are truly in this new realm of light, which Christ has brought into this world, is our response to this commandment to love one another, to love the brethren.

Now John does not put it loosely. Notice his customary blunt language: 'He that saith he is in the light, and hateth his brother, is in darkness even until now. He that loveth his brother abideth in the light, and there is none occasion of stumbling in him.' You see what he means; there is no need of argument about this, it is an absolute test. 'There is no explaining it away on the basis of one's particular disposition,' says John; 'you proclaim and portray exactly what you are by your conduct and behaviour in this respect. If you are not loving your brother, you are still in darkness, and the darkness is within you, whatever you may say. But if you are loving your brother, it is a proof you are truly a Christian in the realm of light, whatever defects you may happen to have.'

Let me put it like this; it is not our intellectual opinion that proclaims truly what we are. You know, it is possible for us to be perfectly orthodox but to be unloving. But your orthodoxy is of no value to you if you do not love your brother; you can talk about this doctrine intellectually, you can be a defender of the faith, and yet the spirit in which you are defending it may be denying the very doctrine you are defending.

This is a terrible test! Orthodoxy is essential, but it is not enough. 'If you are not loving your brother,' says John in effect, 'you are in darkness, you have not the love of Christ.' To love your brother is much more important than orthodoxy; yes, it is more important than mere mechanical correctness in your conduct and behaviour in an ethical sense. There are people who, like the rich young ruler, can say, 'All these things . . .' They are not guilty of the gross sins which they have seen in others, and yet their spirit as they criticise is a portrayal that they do not love their brother. Harshness, the criticising spirit–all that is a negation of this spirit of love. It is something that rises up in my heart and nature and it is, therefore, the proof positive of whether I belong to Him or not. 'If ye know these things,' said the Lord Jesus Christ, 'happy are ye if ye do them' (John 13:17). 'If I,' He also said in effect, in the same passage, 'whom you call Lord and Master, have washed your feet, how much more in a sense ought you to wash one another's feet and be loving towards one another and be anxious to serve one another.' This thing is inevitable–if we belong to Him, we must be manifesting this spirit and type of life.

But let us put it finally in the form of a comparison. Let us just glance at the characteristics of the Christian and the non-Christian in the light of this pronouncement. John puts it very plainly. Let us look at the man who does not love his brother, this unloving kind of person, the man who claims, as these people had claimed, that he is truly Christian. You see, John still has the Gnostics in mind, those people who claimed an unusual knowledge and advancement in the realm of the kingdom of God, but who were denying it by their very attitude towards their brethren whom they despised. 'It is no good boasting of your mystical experiences,' says John; 'what shows whether you are a Christian or not is your attitude towards the brethren. If you love them, you are a Christian.'

Now, what are the things John tells us about unloving people? The first thing is that they are in darkness; that means they belong to the order or realm of the kingdom of darkness. I can do nothing better at this point than to quote the Apostle Paul in Titus 3:3, where he gives this perfect yet terrifying description of the life of the world which is not Christian. This is how he puts it: 'For we ourselves also were sometimes'–that is to say once upon a time–'foolish, disobedient, deceived, serving divers lusts and pleasures, living in malice and envy, hateful, and hating one another.' That is what it means to be in darkness. That, according to the New Testament, is the state of the world outside Christ.

Now you may say that it is not a true description of the world, or of men and women who are not Christians, but I suggest to you that it is a simple and correct account. The world hides itself; there is a superficial charm and manner, there is a superficial culture and chivalry that would conceal this. Yet look at people's faces and listen to what they say about one another, what they say about a person to whom they have recently been so charming and polite. Look at the sneer on their faces–the world is full of this, in spite of all the superficiality. 'Hateful, and hating one another,' selfishness, greed, jealousy, envy, malice, self-centredness–those are the characteristics of the life of the world, the state of being in darkness. And according to John, anyone who is not a Christian is in that position; he is in darkness.

But notice, he puts it like this also: '. . . he that hateth his brother is in darkness, and walketh in darkness, and knoweth not whither he goeth.' This person is not only in that realm of darkness where that is the kind of life and outlook–he is also altogether controlled by that outlook. In other words, the tragedy about the non-Christian is that he is not master of himself or in control of himself; he is governed by his surroundings and circumstances.

Is that not absolutely true? This kind of person is always governed by what is taking place. If things go right, he is happy; he may meet a person whom he likes, and he is happy, but if someone else comes along, he is aroused and angry. It all depends on a sort of accident and chance–whom he meets, what happens to him, what his state and condition is. He has no idea where he is going, no standard, no control; there is no steady policy in his life. He is the victim of the darkness, and thus his life is always uncertain and unreliable.

But let me mention the third thing: '. . . [he] knoweth not whither he goeth, because that darkness hath blinded his eyes.' In other words, because all his trouble is just that he really is blind as to the true nature of life, he has not understood the gospel, he does not realise what is happening to him in this world. He does not realise that he is going on to the next world; he does not know that he has to face God in the judgment; he has not awakened to the whole, real meaning of life. He does not realise that God will ask him about his attitude towards his brother; he is blind to his eternal destiny.

Then the final thing about such a person is that he is a stumbling-block. This is how John puts it: 'He that loveth his brother abideth in the light, and there is none occasion of stumbling in him.' Let me put it like this: The man who is in darkness and who is walking in the darkness and whose mind is dark is an occasion of stumbling both to himself and to everybody else. Because he has this unloving spirit within himself, everything he comes into contact with is going to cause him to stumble, and because he is an unloving person he causes other people to stumble also.

Is this not perfectly true? These people with this unloving nature are always finding problems and troubles. They always see insults where they do not exist; there is always something upsetting them; they are always being put out; they are constantly stumbling because of their unloving spirit. But, says John, they cause other people to stumble also, because as they are in this state and condition no one knows what to do with them. They are always so touchy and sensitive, and they constantly run other people into trouble.

So there is the Apostle's description of the person who does not love his brother; there is this horrible picture of the unloving nature. John gives it in detail, and I have repeated it in detail, trusting that having seen this picture we shall hate it and ask God to forgive us if we have seen anything of ourselves in it.

But let me conclude with a word on the other side. What are Christians, the loving people? They are just the exact opposite of all I have been describing. They are in a different realm–in the light and not in the darkness. They have a purpose governing their lives; they are not dependent upon circumstances and accident and chance; they have a central gospel and a central doctrine. Their eyes have been opened; they have understood the gospel of Jesus Christ, and the result is that there is no occasion of stumbling in them. They do not trip and stumble constantly as they go about the world and meet people, and so other people do not stumble because of them. There is something about them that draws the best out of others.

This is how it works: They are always in the light, they have been enlightened, and they have come to see certain things. Christians have come to see the nature of sin; with the Apostle Paul they have come to see that they were hateful and that they were dwelling in the darkness. They have come to see that the devil had introduced principles into their lives which made them hateful; they were alienated from God. But they realised their danger, and they heard the gospel that offered forgiveness because of the love of God in the Lord Jesus Christ. They saw themselves as hell-deserving sinners who are only saved because of the love of God, and they realise now that this must govern their attitude towards the whole of life.

So they look at their fellow men and women; they see people exactly like themselves before their eyes were opened, and now they are sorry for them. They see that poor person behaving like that because he is a victim of sin; they must be sorry for him and pray that he may see himself and know the love of God in Christ and be delivered out of his sin. They begin to love the hateful person instead of hating him; they say, 'We are all in the same position,' and they begin to have an eye of compassion for them. Their knowledge of the love of God in Christ makes them love other people even as they have been loved themselves. They are new men and women with a new outlook; they are in a new realm. They feel the love of God in their heart, and they want to love Him and glorify Him, and they know they can glorify God most of all by being new men and women, by living as Christ lived and thereby showing and proving that they are indeed true disciples.

Christ our Lord put this perfectly once in a parable of the man who was a servant and was in trouble. He went to his lord and pleaded for forgiveness, and that lord forgave him. But there was another man who was a servant under the first servant who came to him and made exactly the same plea, but he took him by the throat and said, 'No, I won't let you off–you have to pay to the last farthing.' Well, said our Lord (Matt 18:23-35), that man must not think he has been forgiven, for the man who does not forgive will not be forgiven.

What this means is that you and I can only be happy about the fact that we are Christians if we find this loving, forgiving spirit within ourselves. It is idle for us to say that we know that God has forgiven us if we are not loving and forgiving ourselves. People who say they are in the light but who hate and do not forgive their brother are in darkness even now. Men and women who have seen the truth, those who are in the light, have seen themselves and others all under the law of the love of God. And having realised this love which has pardoned them in spite of their unworthiness, they are prepared to do the same to others and to love them and rejoice with them in the same common salvation, in the same common love for the wondrous Lord who 'loved his own . . . unto the end' (John 13:1), even to the Cross and its shame and agony.

'He that abideth in the light loveth his brother, and there is none occasion of stumbling in him.' God grant that as we have examined ourselves in the light of these great pictures we may be able to say with assurance and confidence that we are abiding in the light and loving the brethren.

# 6

# Children, Young Men, and Fathers

I write unto you, little children, because your sins are forgiven you for his name's sake. I write unto you, fathers, because ye have known him that is from the beginning. I write unto you, young men, because ye have overcome the wicked one. I write unto you, little children, because ye have known the Father. I have written unto you, fathers, because ye have known him that is from the beginning. I have written unto you, young men, because ye are strong, and the word of God abideth in you, and ye have overcome the wicked one.

1 JOHN 2:12-14

These three verses come as a kind of parenthesis in the series of appeals and exhortations which the Apostle makes at this particular point in his letter to these early Christians. We have considered the verses in which he tells them that they must keep that commandment of love to the brethren which is so essential to fellowship with God, and he is now proposing to go on to make another great and striking, and to many perhaps, a startling exhortation–'Love not the world, neither the things that are in the world. If any man love the world, the love of the Father is not in him.' But before he does that, he introduces this break, and therefore it is important to discover exactly why the Apostle does this, why he suddenly interrupts his series of exhortations and at the end of verse 11 pauses and says, 'I write unto you, little children, because your sins are forgiven you for his name's sake,' and so on.

Now this is very interesting. The Apostle, as it were, puts it like this: 'I have been showing you,' he says in effect, 'some of the basic principles. I have been reminding you of some of the demands which the Christian life makes upon you; I have been showing you what are the very conditions of blessing.' Why, then, the pause and the break? Well, the answer, it seems to me, is this: it is because the Apostle was a pastor, an understanding and loving pastor. His object after all, as we have seen, was not simply to lay down Christian doctrine; he had a very practical object, which was to help these people. So he has to appeal to them; he wants to make sure that he is carrying them with him; so here, in his typical, practical manner, he just stops for a moment and says, 'Now are you quite clear about all this? You see the line of argument; let me once more just remind you of the thing on which I am basing my whole appeal and exhortation.'

Now that is the way to understand this particular parenthesis. John, at this point, was anxious to do three main things. Firstly, he was anxious to comfort these people; he has been holding forth a very strong and stern doctrine before them–keeping the commandments and loving the brethren–and it is as if he said to himself, 'Now I wonder if these people will be discouraged. Will they feel I am holding the standard so high that they cannot attain to it? Will it make them feel they are condemned sinners and that there is no hope for them at all? Very well, I will just stop and give them a word of comfort.'

The second thing he is anxious to do is to encourage them, and he does so in this way: He, in effect, says to these people, 'Now do not think of this commandment and exhortation of mine as something quite separate or disconnected from anything else. Let me remind you,' says John, 'that all I am saying to you is based upon the fundamental doctrine which I have already outlined to you.' If we were presented with the Christian standard of life and morality and ethics without first of all being shown clearly how this is possible in the light of the Christian doctrine, there would be nothing more discouraging in the world than the New Testament. But, thank God, the New Testament never appeals to us to do anything at all until it has told us certain vital things which are essential to the carrying out of the Christian life; so John writes this to encourage them.

I think he has a third object also, and that is to show them that there is no excuse at all for failure in this life in view of the provision that has been made. In other words, we can look at it like this: Someone may say to me, 'That is all very well! It is an easy thing to tell us to love our brothers; it is a very simple thing to say we are to keep God's commandments; but if you look at them, surely no one can be expected to do these things.' 'But,' says John, 'in the light of my doctrine there is no excuse for failure.' So he introduces this parenthesis in that way; comfort for those who feel condemned, encouragement for those who feel this is some exalted task, and, before he goes any further, taking away every excuse that we may tend to put forward, any attempt to excuse ourselves from this high calling, this great vocation into which we have been called in the Lord Jesus Christ.

John here, as it were, stops and says, 'Do you think it is all hopelessly impossible? Do you think that what I am really asking of you is so heroic as to be entirely outside the reach of the average Christian? It may be possible, you think, for those who go off into monasteries and who spend their whole life in doing nothing but cultivating their religious life, but surely not for the average Christian in business and other affairs. Now,' says John, 'if that is your feeling, it is quite clear to me that you have not grasped the original doctrine. You are approaching the whole thing in the wrong way. Indeed it seems to me that you must be uncertain somewhere as to the basic elements of the Christian faith. So,' he says, 'I am not going to take any risks; I am not going a step further; I shall not make another exhortation until I am perfectly satisfied that we really are agreed about the bases, the fundamentals. It is no use going on with the building if there is something wrong with the foundation.'

And this is the way in which he proceeds to do that: He tells them that he is writing these things to them on a certain assumption: 'I write unto you, little children, *because* your sins are forgiven you for his name's sake. I write unto you, fathers, *because*'–in the light of the fact that–'ye have known him that is from the beginning. I write unto you, young men, *because* ye have overcome the wicked one.' 'That is my basic assumption,' says John, 'and if you are uncertain about that, then obviously these appeals and exhortations of mine will be utterly useless. I shall be wasting my time,' he says, 'if I go on to tell you not to love the world and the things of the world, because unless you are in the basic Christian position you obviously will not understand it and you will feel that the whole thing is a sheer impossibility. So let us go back and just make sure we are agreed about the vital things.' In other words, we have, in these three verses, what I am again describing as the very fundamentals, the bare essentials, the irreducible minimum of the whole Christian position.

Now I shall not go into a detailed discussion as to the mechanics of the way in which John puts this great conspectus of Christian doctrine. You will find that the commentators spend most of their time in doing that–debating as to what exactly John means by 'little children,' 'fathers,' and 'young men' and why he repeats himself as he does. Such discussion is all quite interesting as far as it goes, but it seems to me that it is not very important and not very profitable. Different writers have different views about it, and you will find that it is almost impossible to find two who will agree about this matter. Does 'little children' in verse 1 mean all Christians, or does it literally mean little children–and similarly with 'fathers' and 'young men'? Then in verse 13 it is not the same word in the Greek, and there is a discussion as to whether it means his little children or whether it does not.

We cannot decide all this, and it does not matter. There are two ways of looking at it. You can say that 'little children' means all Christians; he says at the beginning of the chapter, 'My little children, these things write I unto you,' so he is including them all–it is a term of affection from an old man to disciples and followers; that view may well be right. Then there are others who say that there you have all Christians, and then there are two subdivisions–

fathers and young men. Again in verses 12 and 13 he talks about children and once more he divides it into fathers and young men, so the possibility is that he has three divisions. Well, they ask, if that is what he has in mind, why does he put fathers immediately after little children and then young men after that? Would it not be more natural to say, children, young men, fathers?

But I repeat, it does not matter, because what really matters is that clearly the Apostle is telling us that these truths of the Christian life and of the Christian faith must be understood by all of us. At the same time, there are particular emphases that are more important at particular ages and stages. In other words, we must realise that not only the little children are to know that their sins are forgiven–all Christians must know that. It is not only the fathers who know that from the beginning, all Christians should know it. It is not only the young men who overcome the wicked one; that is to be true of all Christians. So that he writes for all, but at the same time there are steps and stages in this Christian life, and at these stages we need one emphasis more than another and then we go on to need another one.

That, to me, is the glory of this Christian faith. The whole is meant for everybody, and yet there are particular applications at particular points, and that, I think, is exactly what John is doing. He is reminding them of the whole position, and as a wise pastor he just has this particular word of emphasis for people in particular ages or stages.

So let us look at it from the particular like this: It is essential that we should be clear about the basic Christian position; there are certain fundamental postulates and assumptions without which it is a sheer waste of time to appeal to people to live the Christian life. That is the New Testament doctrine from beginning to end; it has nothing to say by way of appeal for conduct to anyone who is not a Christian. It is no part of the Christian Church's business to be exhorting the world to practise Christian ethics, for it cannot do it. It is difficult for the Christian, it is impossible for the world, so there is no single ethical exhortation in the Bible to a person who is not standing on the Christian position. Christians do not turn to people of the world and say, 'Love not the world, neither the things that are in the world'; they know they cannot understand the language, still less can they practise it. No, we must be absolutely clear about these fundamental, basic things.

That is why, I think, John repeats these things twice, for repetition is the very art of teaching. Wise teachers always repeat themselves. There are certain things that can never be repeated too often, and although John is an old man, he is a teacher.

So what is it that every Christian should know? What are these basic postulates and assumptions behind the Christian appeal for keeping the commandments, loving the brethren, hating the world, and all the other exhortations? Well, there are just three. First, we must be perfectly clear in our knowledge with regard to the whole question of the forgiveness of sins. 'I write unto you, little children, *because your sins are forgiven you for his name's sake*'–a fundamental postulate.

What does this mean? Let me divide it like this: The first thing that Christians should know is that their sins are forgiven. That can perhaps best be put by a series of negatives. The Christian is not a person who is seeking forgiveness, or who is hoping to be forgiven. The Christian is not a person who is uncertain about forgiveness or who prays for it or tries to merit it. No, Christians are people who *know* that they are forgiven.

Now this is absolutely vital and fundamental. So many people, when you ask them if they know that their sins are forgiven, say, 'I am hoping that they are; I am seeking forgiveness; I am praying for it; I am very uncertain about the whole thing, but I am hoping that my sins will be forgiven me.' 'No!' says John. 'That is not the Christian position–that is a typical non-Christian statement. The Christian is one whose sins are already forgiven.'

Let me emphasise that still more. The Christian's certainty and assurance of forgiveness of sins is based upon his knowledge of the *way* in which his sins are forgiven–'I write unto you, little children, because your sins are forgiven you *for his name's sake*.' What a glorious statement! You know, the whole of the Christian doctrine in its fundamentals is there. He is everything. This is the basis of our certainty and assurance; we are forgiven because of the perfect, the finished, the full work of the Lord Jesus Christ on our behalf.

Christians know that their sins are forgiven, not because they bank loosely and vaguely upon the love of God, still less because they rest upon the hope of their own good lives and merits or their own good works.

Again, this is absolutely central. Let us ask ourselves the question, Have I believed my sins are forgiven; and if so, on what grounds do I believe? Now you put that question and you will find that people say, 'I believe my sins are forgiven because God is love.' Yes, but if those are your grounds for believing, then I ask again, where does the Lord Jesus Christ come in? Is He central? He is central with John because 'your sins are forgiven you for his name's sake.'

John has already put that like this in verses 1 and 2: 'If any man sin, we have an advocate with the Father, Jesus Christ the righteous: and he is the propitiation for our sins: and not for ours only, but also for the sins of the whole world.' Christians have certain objective grounds for their assurance of forgiveness of sin. Let me summarise them again. It is 'for his name's sake.' What makes me know my sins are forgiven is that the Lord Jesus Christ is standing there as my representative with God; it is for His sake, for His name's sake, that I am forgiven. My sin has been dealt with in Him–'The Lord hath laid on him the iniquity of us all,' and 'with his stripes we are healed' (Isa 53:6-5). Our sins have been taken and laid upon the Lord Jesus Christ by God Himself; and because He has borne the punishment of my sins, I shall not bear the punishment for them because my sins are forgiven in Him, for His name's sake. As we saw in our consideration of Chapter 1, 'If we confess our sins, he is faithful and just to forgive us our sins,' because the very justice of God insists upon my being forgiven, because Christ has been punished for me. These are the grounds of my certainty and assurance.[1]

But let me rather put it in this practical form–and I do not hesitate to put it like this: if you are uncertain about the forgiveness of your sins, that in itself is sin. I want to be ruthless about this because there are people who feel that an assurance of forgiveness of sins is presumption, and they rather give the impression that they are being humble and modest. They say, 'I would not like to say my sins are forgiven, I do not feel good enough to say that, I am so conscious of my own unworthiness.' They give the impression that they have unusual lowliness and humility.

The simple reply to that is that if you speak in that way there is only one explanation of it, and that is lack of faith, that is unbelief; it is no mark of saintliness to be uncertain that your sins are forgiven; it is to deny and doubt the Word of God. The certainty of the New Testament is that your sins are forgiven you; you have been forgiven for His name's sake. If you, therefore, do not know that, it is because you are not clear about the doctrine, because you are still relying upon yourself, because you are not relying upon the finished, complete work of the Son of God for you upon the cross. It is because you do not realise the merit and the power of His blessed name. That name pleaded before God immediately assures pardon–the name that is above every other name, the name in whom all fulness dwells, the name that gives an entry to the courts of heaven and to the very presence of God.

So let us be quite clear about this. It is absolutely essential to living the Christian life, because while you are unhappy or disturbed about this question of forgiveness of sins, you cannot be going forward; in a sense there is no point in going forward. What is the point of my saying to myself, 'Well, from now on, I am going to live the Christian life, I am going to try to keep the commandments,' if I am uncertain about my past sins? Though I may live a good life from now on, the past guilt remains. How can I go on until that has been dealt with? And the only way to deal with it is to believe on the Lord Jesus Christ. You cannot undo what you have done, you cannot go back and erase your past–it is impossible. But it has been done in Christ, and I say once more with John that there is no point appealing to people to go forward until they are clear about the past.

Are you clear about it? Do you know that the Lord Jesus Christ has borne your sins and has died your death and risen again to justify you, and are you relying utterly and absolutely upon Him and upon Him alone? If so, you can say that you know your sins are forgiven you. That is the first thing that every Christian should know.

The second is that every Christian should know the way in which sin can be overcome. 'I write unto you, young men, because ye have overcome the wicked one' (v 13), and 'I have written unto you, young men, because ye are strong, and the word of God abideth in you, and ye have overcome the wicked one' (v 14). Again I would call attention to the way in which John puts it. 'I write unto you, young men, because *ye have overcome*'–not because you are going to, but because you have.

Now what does this mean? Well, it can be put very briefly like this. There is an immediate victory of which one becomes conscious the moment one believes on the Lord Jesus Christ. Let no one misunderstand me. I spend a good deal of time denouncing the gospel of perfection, and I am as far from preaching it as I have ever been, but I say this: the moment we believe on the Lord Jesus Christ, we are conscious of a victory over the wicked one–not complete absolute victory, but victory. We may still be conscious of great weakness, yes, but the moment we believe on Christ we have an immediate consciousness that we are somehow or other no longer under the dominion of sin. Yes, the wicked one is very great; he is very powerful and we may be afraid of him in our weakness, and yet we know that there is something about us, there is an immediate victory. Though we have not finished with sin, we are no longer under the dominion of sin and Satan. We may be conscious of great weakness, and yet we know that he is a defeated enemy and that we are fools if we listen to him.

But to put it still more simply, we can say that those who believe on the Lord Jesus Christ know that they are in Christ; they know that Christ has already defeated the wicked one. It is a great thing when you are confronted by an enemy to know that that enemy is defeated. That is the position of Christian men and women; they cannot be beaten by the enemy in combat because there is Someone standing by them who has done it. You are a little child in the victorious army, and you can leave the enemy to Him.

That is the way to understand this victory over sin. John divides it like this: we know we have been made strong. 'I have written unto you, young men, because ye are strong'–it does not mean that they are strong in and of themselves, or that they have developed some strange, mystic strength. Rather it must be that they know they have been made strong. Every Christian should know that, and we know it like this: We receive new life and power; the moment we believe on the Lord Jesus Christ and become Christians, we are aware of a change and of a difference. We know that something has come into us, something has happened to us, there has been a kind of infusion of new life, we are aware of a power that we never knew before. There is strength, though it may be small, which we never had in the past. So we can see why John has this parenthesis. What is the point of telling us to keep the commandments and to love the brethren and to hate the world unless we have been given strength?

Furthermore, '*the word of God abideth in you.*' The word of God is the word which brings new life to us. 'Being born again,' says Peter, 'not of corruptible seed, but of incorruptible, by the word of God, which liveth and abideth for ever' (1 Pet 1:23). James talks about this life being *engrafted* into us by the word (Jas 1:21). The word of God comes into us and gives us life, and it abides and the life grows. We can think of this word also as the 'sword of the Spirit.' Paul, when he tells the Ephesians to put on the whole armour of God, gives a list, and he refers to the 'sword of the Spirit' with which we are to fight the enemy–'the sword of the Spirit, which is the word of God' (Eph 6:17).

How is it that this word of God makes us strong to fight sin? I think it does it in this way: it shows me the horrible nature of sin; and while the word of God abides in me, I am made to see sin in all its ugliness and selfishness and perversion and I hate it. It also teaches men and women about the destiny of those who are the slaves of sin. It shows them that they are going to hell and destruction outside the life of God for all eternity. It also shows them, thank God, the power of Christ and how Christ has defeated the enemy already and how Christ comes into them and makes them strong and enables them to become more than conquerors against all these things that assail them.

Let me sum it up again like this: If we feel that the demands of this Christian life are too high or impossible, it is nothing but sheer ignorance, a sheer lack of faith. If we feel that we would rather be talking about our own weakness and about our own failures, then let me emphasise once more that that is not humility, nor Christian modesty; it is lack of faith and lack of knowledge. There is a sense in which we have no right to be weak, no business to be failures when all this is offered to us. 'So then,' says John, 'I am writing to you because you know these things and because you know that these things are facts.' So the Christian must have this certain knowledge of the power of Christ and the ability to overcome sin.

And that brings me to the third and last point, which is that we must all have a knowledge of the Father and of the Son. This, as we have seen, is the basic truth in the whole epistle. 'I write unto you, fathers, because ye have known him that is from the beginning'–that is, the Lord Jesus Christ: 'That which was from the beginning, which we have heard, which we have seen with our eyes, which we have looked upon, and our hands have handled, of the Word of life' (1:1). Then: 'I write unto you, little children, because ye have known the Father.' This is the blessed knowledge that every Christian must have, a knowledge of God–not God as some great power, not as some great force, not someone who is opposed to us and hates us, imposing these commandments upon us–but God as Father, God who has loved us with an everlasting love, the God and Father of our Lord Jesus Christ.

This the God who so loves us that He counts the very hairs of our head, the God who causes the sun to rise upon this world, this amazing Father God. 'We know Him,' says John. 'I write to you because you know Him, and if you know Him you will not feel that His commandments are a sacrifice; you will know that are all destined for your good; you will know He has brought them in because He wants to bless you and because He wants you to be conformed to the image of His own dear Son.' So it is a knowledge of the Father and likewise a knowledge of the Lord Jesus Christ; to know Him in person, to know His work for us, to know Him in His offices as the sin-bearer, as the sacrifice, as the prophet, priest, and King. It is to know the New Testament doctrine concerning Him, and above all to know Him and to feel that He is near in the hour of need and in temptation so that we can rise above it; to know perfect peace in Him and through Him; to know the Father and to know the Son.

There, then, are the three basic things which every Christian must know: sins forgiven for His name's sake, power to overcome the sin, and to know God the Father and God the Son through God the Holy Spirit.

This is the knowledge that John also applies in particular to the different age groups. While we are young in this Christian faith and feel so weak and small, the one thing we really want to know is that God is our Father, that God loves us and that our sins are forgiven; so he emphasises that in writing to the 'little children.' You see, in that first stage all we really want to know is that we can, as it were, recline in safety in the loving arms of God. That is what the child wants; he depends upon the parent; he wants to receive everything, but he does not give anything, and God is like that with us, in the early stages. At the beginning of the Christian life we do not understand much, so God gives us everything.

I have often said in passing, and I am sure every minister and preacher will confirm what I say, that as a man goes on preaching this gospel, he finds he has to work more and more. In the early days of my Christian ministry I was given sermons, but now I have to work harder, and it is like that in the Christian life. God is the Father, and the child is given everything. Little children, you know your sins are forgiven you.

Yes, but go on a little bit and you become a young man; you find now there is a fight involved, and 'young men' in the Christian life are conscious of that fight, and the enemy is attacking them. In the beginning the Christian life was easy; now there is a conflict and difficulties. 'You are quite right,' says John, 'and what I would emphasise for you is this: He can make you strong, and you can overcome the wicked one, and the word of God will abide in you, so that when you are in this middle stage of the Christian life you have to remember this–the young man, the middle age group, must especially hold on to this–that you are not left to yourself. The word of God abides in you, and Christ who has defeated the enemy can enable you to overcome. And, fathers, you who are old in age, some old in the Christian life, what should be true of you is this:

you no longer as children must expect everything to come automatically. You are not in the stage to fight combats and conflicts. No, you have gone beyond that, you should have gone beyond it, you no longer are interested in the gifts, no longer interested in the fight, though you are still fighting. What matters to you is the knowledge of the giver Himself. You are old, and you know you have not much longer in this world, and what should be occupying your mind and attention is that the day will soon come when you will see Him face to face. You know him that is from the beginning. Do you dwell more and more on Him? As a child you thought of gifts; you now are thinking more of the giver. You have gone through the struggles, and you have overcome; you know all about that; now what you are thinking about is the consummation, the ultimate reward, of standing and seeing Him face to face. So you dwell more and more upon the person, and you say, "Oh, what I long for is to know Him better; to know my Saviour as a person and to know God better." And you look wistfully to the day when with Paul you will be able to say, "To me to live is Christ, and to die is gain" (Phil 1:21), for it means "to be with Christ; which is far better' (Phil 1:23).

There are steps and stages like that in the Christian life and whatever stage we are in, there is an aspect of the truth that speaks specifically and especially to us, some basic doctrine for us all and a special word of encouragement according to our several positions. Let us thank God that He caused His servant, the Apostle, to pause at this point to introduce this glorious, magnificent parenthesis. Let us thank God that we stand on such solid ground: a knowledge of sin forgiven, a knowledge of how to overcome sin, and above all the knowledge of Himself, God the Father, God the Son, and God the Holy Ghost.

# 7

# The Love of the World

Love not the world, neither the things that are in the world. If any man love the world, the love of the Father is not in him. For all that is in the world, the lust of the flesh, and the lust of the eyes, and the pride of life, is not of the Father, but is of the world. And the world passeth away, and the lust thereof: but he that doeth the will of God abideth for ever.

1 JOHN 2:15-17

We find here the Apostle resuming the list of practical injunctions and exhortations which he was giving to these people, after having interrupted this list in order to remind them of their resources. He is anxious that they should understand clearly that he is not asking the impossible, nor is he raising the standard too high. Their sins are already forgiven them; they have the strength and the power whereby they can overcome; and they know God and have fellowship with Him and the Lord Jesus Christ. So it is in the light of these things that he exhorts them in this way to put certain principles into practice.

Now here in these verses we have a great negative exhortation. Having told them what they are to do, he here reminds them of something that they are to avoid–'Love not the world.' As we are to love God and keep His commandments, as we are to love the brethren, so, equally definitely, we are not to love the world, neither the things that are in the world. And this is something that follows quite logically and inevitably from what he has already been saying. This negative is vitally important; it is quite as important as the positive, and I think we can agree in saying that there are no more solemn words addressed to Christian people anywhere in the Scriptures than these.

It behooves us, therefore, to approach them carefully lest we misunderstand them, because I believe it is equally true to say that there are perhaps no words which have been so frequently misunderstood and misinterpreted as these. I think the explanation of that is that we all have a tendency to engage in self-defence, and the danger is to approach these words and to interpret them in such a way as to make me all right and probably condemn other people. We are all experts at rationalising our sins and explaining away what we do, and it is interesting to hear how people often quote these verses, fondly imagining that they are perfectly all right themselves with regard to these words and yet who often display in their lives that they have certainly completely misunderstood one of the main emphases of this particular injunction. We must approach it, therefore, with an open mind, and we must take the words as they stand.

There have been two main misinterpretations of this injunction. The first is what I would call the *ascetic* interpretation, which says that these words mean that Christians literally have to go out of the world and segregate themselves from society. This is the misinterpretation which led to monasticism and to the whole tendency to go out of the world and to live what is called the 'religious life'—people divide Christians up into the 'religious' and the 'lay,' or the 'religious' and the 'secular,' as if living within the confines of some kind of institution or order were a guarantee that one would no longer love the world or the things that are in it.

The second misinterpretation is the one I would describe as the *incomplete* or *partial* interpretation of these words. Instead of taking John's words as they are, people say, 'We must not be guilty of worldliness,' and then they proceed to define worldliness as they think of it and not as John thinks of it. Their conception of worldliness is a small one, and they fail to face John's full exposition of it here.

There are two main subdivisions of this incomplete or partial interpretation. The first says, 'We will not go to dances or to cinemas. We will give up smoking, we will not go to theatres, we will give up gambling and a few other things like that.' The moment these people talk about worldliness, that is all they think about; they are not guilty of certain things and therefore they feel that they are not guilty of the charge of worldliness.

Secondly, there are those who really seem to think that worldliness just means being interested in politics and social activities. They say, 'No Christian should ever be concerned about political matters because that is of the world, and the Christian is not to love such things.' So as long as they take no interest in political and social questions, they feel they are not guilty of worldliness. But they ignore completely, as I hope to show you, the Apostle's interpretation of what exactly is meant by loving the world and the things that are in the world.

Now I feel that this is of very great importance. One often hears people talking eloquently, and with much feeling, about worldliness and denouncing it, and one realises at once that they have only taken one little section and have completely ignored the remainder. I say again that the cause of that–and we are all subject to it–is this instinct of self-defence; we introduce our definition to guarantee that we are all right and others may be wrong, but that is not the Scriptural definition of what is meant by worldliness. So we must face these words with unusual interest; we must come before them without preconceived notions and ideas, and we must look at them as they are; we must allow them to search and examine us in order that we may know truly and exactly what worldliness really is. As we do so, of course, we shall discover exactly where we are and where we stand. It is a searching and very serious word as I have said; there is no word that so examines us down to the very depths of our being as a word like this.

Not only that, it is a word that again reminds us of something that is absolutely essential to the enjoyment of the fellowship of the Father and of the Son. There are so many people within the

Christian world who are unhappy in their Christian life and who are not getting the benefits and enjoyment simply because they have not faced a text like this; they have not allowed it to search them and influence their whole life. So let us approach it in this way.

First of all, let us ask what John means by this injunction. Well, the first thing to ask, obviously, is this: what is '*the world*' in this case? Now I think it is important that we should agree that he is not referring here to creation as such; he is not thinking of the mountains and the valleys and the rivers, the streams and the sun and the moon and the stars; he does not mean the physical world in that sense. There are people who have even thought that to 'love not the world, neither the things that are in the world' means to shut one's eyes to the glory and the beauty of nature.

But it does not mean that; neither does it mean the life of the world in general. It does not mean family relationships, though there are people who have misinterpreted it like that; they have often regarded marriage as sinful. Not once but very often in my ministerial life have I had to deal with nice, sincere Christian people who have solemnly believed, through misinterpreting a text like this, that Christian people should not marry. Their reason is that marriage involves certain relationships which they regard as sinful; they would regard the very gift of sex as being sinful in and of itself.

So the 'world' does not mean creation; it does not mean family relationships; it is not the state; it does not mean engaging in business or a profession or all these things which are essential to life; it does not mean government and authorities and powers, for all these have been ordained by God Himself. So there is nothing so grievous as to misinterpret 'the world' in some such terms as that.

What, then, does it mean? Clearly the very text and the whole teaching of the Bible shows that it must mean the organisation and the mind and the outlook of mankind as it ignores God and does not recognise him and as it lives a life independent of Him, a life that is based upon this world and this life only. It means the outlook that has rebelled against God and turned its back upon Him. It means, in other words, the typical kind of life that is being lived by the average person today, who has no thought of God, but thinks only of this world and life, who thinks in terms of time and is governed by certain instincts and desires. It is the whole outlook upon life that is exclusive of God.

What, secondly, are the characteristics of that kind of life? Well, fortunately John answers that question in verse 16. First verse 15 says, 'Love not the world, neither the things that are in the world. If any man love the world, the love of the Father is not in him. For'– there it is–'all that is in the world, the lust of the flesh, and the lust of the eyes, and the pride of life, is not of the Father, but is of the world.' Now '*lust*' means an inordinate affection or desire; lust means the abuse of something which is naturally and perfectly right and legitimate in and of itself. Paul, I think, puts this perfectly in his first letter to the Corinthians when he tells us to use this world and not abuse it (1 Cor 7:31), and to abuse it means we are guilty of lust. Lust, in other words, means that instead of controlling our desires and using them as we ought to, we are controlled by them; they master us and they control us. There are certain desires in us that are perfectly legitimate, they have been given by God. Yes, but if we are governed and controlled by them and our whole outlook upon life is circumscribed by these things, then we are guilty of lust; that is the meaning of the word.

The Apostle mentions 'the lust of *the flesh*.' What does this tell us? Well, here John is talking about lust in the sense that it arises from and appertains to nature, belonging as such to our physical bodies. Now we are living in an age when people say they believe in plain speaking; therefore let us put it quite plainly. This is his definition of sensuality; he is talking about the kind of person who lives only for sensual gratification. That includes the kind of man or woman who lives to eat; the lust for food, people whose whole outlook seems to be just that–their interest in food and drink–the expert knowledge they have on drink! How they delight to talk about it and call themselves connoisseurs and experts in tastes and flavours, living for eating and drinking. Now the hunger instinct is perfectly legitimate; we have to eat in order to live; but if you live to eat, you are guilty of the lust of the flesh, and it is exactly the same with drinking. If it is your controlling and main interest in life, it is a lust.

The same applies to sex. I need not labour these things; you have only to look at the newspapers and journals and you see the whole thing shouting and blaring at you; the world seems to be full of it. These clever, subtle businessmen who produce the newspapers and magazines know exactly what appeals to the public palate, so they put these things always in the forefront, and they all belong to this lust of the flesh–the abuse of certain natural instincts and desires that are a part of human nature and life. Do not love that, says John, do not be guilty of that, do not be controlled by that sort of thing; that has nothing to do with this godly life, it is the very antithesis of it.

But let us go on; not only 'the lust of the flesh,' but also 'the lust of *the eye*.' The best way of defining this is to say that it is the kind of man or woman who lives according to false values. They judge by appearances and by outward show. This, of course, often leads to the one we have already dealt with. It is through the eyes that so often sin arises; it is what we see and what the world makes us see that so often makes us sin. That is a large subject, and I can only just touch upon it in passing, but it no doubt includes sin when it is in the intellectual stage. Our Lord put it in this way: 'Whosoever looketh on a woman . . .' (Matt 5:28). The lust of the eyes includes that; it is a kind of invidious looking, sin in the intellect, the toying and playing with it in the imagination and thought. But it does not stop at that; the lust of the eyes means also a kind of vanity which delights in pomp and mighty splendour, in an appearance, in anything that appeals to the eyes. How full the world is of this kind of thing–mighty pomp and show, merely the appearance, giving an impression.

This pleases also the people whose main interest in life is their personal appearance. I am trying to speak of these things dispassionately, but it seems to me that there is nothing which is sadder in the world than people who just live for their own personal appearance and the impression that it makes. Clothing–oh, the time and the energy and the enthusiasm that goes into this! The talking and the writing; again you see it shouting at you everywhere. But you get it equally with certain people in the matter of their house and home. The lust of the eyes–how pathetic it is that human beings, endowed with the faculties that God has given, can live for things like that, this outlook of pomp and appearance and show. It is sad, too, to think how this often enters into the realm of the Church; you find people are dressing up in vestments all for processions and appearances–the lust of the eyes, the outward show.

The next step that John introduces is what he calls '*the pride of life.*' The best way to define this is to call it self-glorification, a very subtle thing. This is something that perhaps we can divide into two sections; it includes ambition, and it includes contempt of others; 'the pride of life' means a pride in oneself generally at the expense of someone else, glorifying in something that is true of oneself in this life and world, something, in a sense, that has nothing to do with the soul and spirit of man. Let me analyse it a little: pride of birth, pride in your family, pride in your industry, proud that you have a particular name or that there is particular blood in you, so-called pride in social status. How men brag about this! Pride in influence, the people we know, our acquaintances! People love all this sort of thing; they are anxious to get into certain circles, anxious to belong to a certain club; but it has nothing to do with the soul, nothing to do with the spirit, nothing to do with God and His honour and glory! How men and women give their thought to this kind of thing; and oh, the money they spend on it, the time and the energy, the way they suffer, the jealousy and envy which arises–the pride of life!

Then there is the question of wealth, the way people pride themselves on their wealth and their material possessions. The pride of life as it shows itself in the school to which you went–a little better than somebody else's school, the college you attend, the university you belong to–how this influences life! There is a sense of superiority and a despising of others, feeling rather sorry for others. 'Where do they come from?' people ask.

Now I go into these things in detail because this kind of thing creeps into the life of the Christian Church. This is the sort of thing one often hears in Christian circles; these are the standards of judgement rather than spirituality–pride in knowledge and learning, ability and culture and erudition. Man boasts of his brain, his knowledge and his understanding; it is just a part of this pride. It is a striving for worldly honours, and, let me be quite honest again, not only worldly honours, but often ecclesiastical honours also. It is part of the pride of life, this ambition to get on and succeed, to be greater than someone else, this idea of self-glorification in some shape or form. And that, according to the Apostle John, is what is meant by 'Love not the world, neither the things that are in the world.'

Now I do not know whether he intended to give a comprehensive definition, but it does seem to me that in his third statement John really does cover the entire field. But let me emphasise this. There is an order in the three steps–the lust of the flesh, the lust of the eyes, the pride of life–the body, the soul and the spirit–and I am putting it like this in order to bring out this particular emphasis, that there may be no question whatsoever that the most serious and the most terrible of the three is the third, the pride of life. It is not for us to make comparisons in these things, but I think the Bible does teach us that the sins of the spirit are always worse than the sins of the flesh. There is something more or less natural about the sins of the flesh in one sense, but the sin of the spirit is the thing that is most opposed of all to the life of Christ and that which was manifested in Him. Let us be careful, therefore, that in denouncing the sins of the flesh we are not at the same time guilty of the pride of life, which is worse. Let us be careful, when we say we are not guilty because we do not do certain things, that we are not proud and despise others because of birth or position or university or one of these other things. It is as you go up in the scale from the body to the spirit that the sin becomes more and more subtle and more and more harmful to the true Christian life.

Next, why should we not love the world and the things that are in the world? Why is it of vital importance that we keep this injunction? John puts it like this: not to obey this commandment means a denial of our love to God and of our knowledge of Him. 'If any man love the world, the love of the Father is not in him,' says John; 'If you love these other things, they are incompatible; you cannot serve God and mammon; you cannot love God and the world at the same time.' 'Whosoever therefore will be a friend of the world is the enemy of God,' says the Apostle James (4:4). It is an utter denial of what we claim to believe.

Consider, then, the second reason: Love of the world and the things of the world is a denial of the life that is in us. 'For all that is in the world, the lust of the flesh, and the lust of the eyes, and the pride of life, is not of the Father, but is of the world,' and the word 'of' there means that it is not derived from, it does not originate in the Father. Christians, according to the Apostle's definition, as we have seen, are people who have in them the life of Christ–Christ dwelling and living in them. Therefore, says John, if you claim that Christ is dwelling within you, you cannot be guilty of loving the things that arise from the lust of the flesh and the lust of the eyes and the pride of life. Look at Him; He was never guilty of those sins of the flesh. He did not believe in outward pomp and show and appearance. No, He was meek and lowly; He was someone who was the very antithesis of all the loudness and vulgarity of the world and its delight in appearance and mere show. And when you come to this question of the pride of life, why, you see it still more definitely. He lived with very poor parents; He was born in a stable, and His cradle was nothing but a manger. He worked with His hands as a carpenter, a manual labourer, and that is the Lord of glory, the Saviour of our soul! That is the life which we claim is in us.

And what was His teaching? 'Blessed are the meek'; the very opposite of the so-called worldly type of person. 'Blessed are the poor in spirit'; not those who are proud and arrogant and ambitious and who look down upon others because of certain things. No, 'poor in spirit,' feeling that they are unworthy and that they have nothing at all. 'Blessed are they which do hunger and thirst after righteousness'–that is His teaching (Matt 5:5, 3, 6). 'The Son of Man came not to be ministered unto, but to minister, and to give his life a ransom for many' (Matt 20:28). In the world the great lord it over others; it is not so in His kingdom: '. . . he that is greatest among you shall be your servant,' said our Lord (Matt 23:11). He was the friend of publicans and sinners, and He was much misunderstood because of that. In other words, the great characteristic of our Lord was that He was interested in people's souls. He did not look at their clothing, or at their birth or ancestry or possessions. He valued the soul that was there, and that is true of all His followers. Paul puts it like this: 'Henceforth know we no man after the flesh; yea, though we have known Christ after the flesh, yet now henceforth know we him no more' (2 Cor 5:16). Or again, he said, 'There is neither Jew nor Greek, there is neither bond nor free, there is neither male nor female: for ye are all one in Christ Jesus' (Gal 3:28). All these things are demolished; the soul is what matters, not these other things.

In other words, Christians have an entirely different conception of all these things from the man of the world; the birth that Christians know is the rebirth, not natural birth; the wealth they are interested in is the wealth of the riches of glory; the knowledge they aspire after is not human knowledge, but the knowledge of God. The associations of which they are proud are not those which you find in noble circles; it is the people of God, it is the Christian Church, the saints, however humble and lowly they may chance to be. The honour that they crave for is not the honour of a great name amongst men, but the honour of being known by God and of anticipating the day when they shall hear the blessed words, 'Well done, thou good and faithful servant . . . enter thou into the joy of thy Lord' (Matt 25:21).

All that is the very opposite, the antithesis, of that which is so true of the world. Christians can say with the Apostle Paul, 'God forbid that I should glory, save in the cross of our Lord Jesus Christ' (Gal 6:14). God forbid that I should boast of anything but that; not my birth, not my appearance, not my knowledge, not my understanding, not my wealth, not my social status, nothing! 'God forbid that I should glory, save in the cross of our Lord Jesus Christ by whom the world is crucified unto me, and I unto the world.'

But the last reason given by John for not loving the world is that if we love the world, it means we do not truly understand this great gospel of salvation. 'The world passeth away,' says John, 'and the lust thereof: but he that doeth the will of God abideth for ever.' What he means is this: if you still love the world and the things that are in it, then it is clear that you have never understood the principles of sin. Cannot you see that all that belongs to the world is passing away? All these things, says John, are disappearing, they are dying. You may be proud of your personal appearance, but you will soon be old and haggard. You will be dying, and then you will have nothing to boast of, it is all passing. Oh fool, to glory in something that is so transient! Wealth, riches, learning, knowledge, social status and all these things, they are vanishing, they have the seeds of death in them. Christian people, how can we glory in things like that? It means we are blind to our own gospel which starts by telling us that all that is under the wrath of God and will be destroyed. It is all going to perdition and eternal destruction; so those who live for these things, therefore, are utterly inconsistent and show that they have never understood that if they belong to that realm they will be destroyed to all eternity. They must come out of and escape from it, and they should glory in the fact that there is a new life and realm, a new kingdom, and if they belong to this, they will abide for ever.

'So,' says the Apostle, 'that is my injunction to you; realise these truths; do the will of God; do not be concerned about your own desires. Do the will of God, and if you do that, you will abide for ever. You will be building up a firm foundation, a building which will be tried and tested as by fire, but because it consists of gold and precious metals and not of wood, hay and stubble, it will last and it will stand the test. And when you arrive in glory, your works will follow you and you will rest in eternal joy from your labours.'

# 8

# The Antichrist

Little children, it is the last time: and as ye have heard that antichrist shall come, even now are there many antichrists; whereby we know that it is the last time. They went out from us, but they were not of us; for if they had been of us, they would no doubt have continued with us: but they went out, that they might be made manifest that they were not all of us. . . . Who is a liar but he that denieth that Jesus is the Christ? He is antichrist, that denieth the Father and the Son. Whosoever denieth the Son, the same hath not the Father: but he that acknowledgeth the Son hath the Father also.

1 JOHN 2:18-19, 22-23

It is important for us to realise that these verses must be taken in the context of the whole section which runs from verse 18 to verse 28. Furthermore, even before we come to analyse the section, it is also important that we should realise the connection between it and what has gone before. The Apostle's theme is that we must always bear in mind that, placed as we are in this difficult and trying world, the great thing which is offered us by the Christian gospel is fellowship and communion with God, God the Father and God the Son through the Holy Spirit. So having laid down the basis of the fellowship, he has then gone on to tell them of certain things that may rob them of that fellowship, and we have looked at these.

Then having said all that he now goes on to this further statement, but how do we fit it into the scheme? Well, so far the Apostle has been dealing with certain things within ourselves that tend to interrupt the fellowship–my failure to keep the commandments or to love my brethren; my failure to observe this injunction of not loving the world and living according to its mentality and outlook–all that, in a sense, is addressed to certain possibilities of failure resident within the Christian believer. 'But,' says John, 'unfortunately we cannot stop at that point; the dangers besetting us not only arise from within, there are certain dangers also outside us.' And what he deals with in this particular section is the great danger that ever confronts us as Christian people, arising, as it were, in the very atmosphere in which we live. Indeed, the danger which he emphasises here is the danger that arises in and from the life of the Church herself.

In other words, we have not only certain things to watch as individual Christians; but also collectively, as Christian people, we have to be very wary of certain common, general dangers to which we are subject as members of the Church; and that is the theme with which he deals here. There is a great enemy outside us who, as he tells us later on in this section, is trying to seduce us, and he says in verse 26, 'These things have I written unto you concerning them that seduce you'– those who would lead you astray, those who would entice you away from the real truth itself to something which is not actually the truth although it looks like it. It is the danger of being led astray by the great power that is amongst us and which is out for our destruction and for the destruction of the entire Christian Church. That is the theme of this section from verses 18 to 28. You can see it follows very logically from the previous exhortations; he goes from us, ourselves, to the whole atmosphere in which we live.

Now for the sake of clarity of thought and understanding let me suggest to you the way in which this section should be divided up. There are three great points in this whole exhortation; the first is the importance of realising the nature or the character of the spiritual conflict in which we find ourselves. This is the theme of verses 18 and 19 and partly also of verses 22 and 23.

The second theme is the way whereby we may realise this danger; that is the special message of verses 20 and 21 and 27, where you find this: 'But ye have an unction from the Holy One, and ye know all things. I have not written unto you because ye know not the truth, but because ye know it, and that no lie is of the truth. . . . But the anointing which ye have received of him abideth in you, and ye need not that any man teach you: but as the same anointing teacheth you of all things, and is truth, and is no lie, and even as it hath taught you, ye shall abide in him.' This is the great doctrine of the anointing and the unction which is possessed by every true Christian believer.

And then the third theme is the way to avoid the dangers that arise from this mighty spiritual conflict in which we find ourselves, and that is the theme of the remaining verses of the section. These then are the three great matters: realising the danger; the faculty and the power that are given unto us by God to enable us to realise it; and the way to fight against it, to avoid it, and to be delivered from all its terrible consequences.

This, you will see at once, is a theme that one meets with quite frequently in the New Testament. There are many other instances of it; you will find it for instance in 2 Peter 2, where Peter deals with exactly the same thing. But a classic example of this is Ephesians 6, where Paul talks about putting on 'the whole armor of God'–and why?–because 'we wrestle not against flesh and blood, but against principalities, against powers . . . against spiritual wickedness in high places' (Eph 6:11-12). And, of course, the book of Revelation is in a sense a book which is entirely devoted to this particular matter. In other words, the New Testament is full of this great question of the spiritual conflict in which we find ourselves as Christian people.

Now at this point I want to consider only the first section–the importance of realising the nature of this conflict in which we find ourselves. 'Little children, it is the last time: and as ye have heard that antichrist shall come, even now are there many antichrists; whereby we know that it is the last time. They went out from us, but they were not of us; for if they had been of us, they would no doubt have continued with us: but they went out, that they might be made manifest that they were not all of us.'

It seems to me that we have two things to do in order to understand what John means here. First, we have to try to understand these terms. What is he warning us about? Secondly, we must relate this danger with which we are confronted to our present experience. How are we going to react to it; what are we going to do about it? Obviously the Apostle deals with it because it was something that was discouraging to these first Christians, and it is a matter that still tends to discourage people. So it is vitally important that we should not only understand the problem, but also that we should be quite clear that we are relating ourselves correctly to it.

So let us first of all look at the very terms which the Apostle uses. He starts by saying that this is '*the last time*,' or *a* last time. Here again is a phrase that you will find in many places in the New Testament. For instance, the Apostle Paul, in writing to Timothy, says, 'In the last days perilous times shall come' (2 Tim 3:1). Or again, 'God, who . . . spake in time past,' says the author of the epistle to the Hebrews, 'unto the fathers by the prophets, hath in these last days spoken unto us by his Son' (Heb 1:1). These are the terms which are characteristic of the New Testament and its teaching; so it is all-important that we should understand exactly what they mean.

Of course there are some who think that this is no problem at all. They say that it is just part of the general error of which the Apostle and those first Christians were all guilty. They thought that the Lord was going to return in their time and generation; they all fell into the same trap, and John here really was just saying, 'You have only a few years left in this world, because it is soon coming to an end–it is the last time.' 'All of them,' say these people, 'fell into that particular error, but looked at from the twentieth century with all its enlightenment and especially in view of the higher criticism of the last century which has thrown such light upon these problems, there is no difficulty.'

But that is much too simple an explanation; the New Testament teaching itself prohibits us from explaining it in that way. Take, for instance, 2 Thessalonians 2, where Paul goes out of his way to teach the Thessalonians that quite obviously we are not to expect the return of the Lord at any moment. He says that certain things have to take place before the day of the Lord will come. He warns them that there may be a great interval, that there is going to be a great apostasy. 'It is not coming as quickly as you think,' he says; so he immediately counteracts that tendency, and there are many other passages in the New Testament that do exactly the same thing. Indeed, the book of Revelation alone, the Apocalypse, is sufficient in and of itself to show this cannot be dismissed as just that common error of imagining that the Lord's return was at hand.

No, it seems to me that when we put together all the New Testament uses of these phrases, we are driven to some such conclusion as this: The whole period from the coming of our Lord, and especially from His death and resurrection and ascension and the descent of the Holy Spirit on the day of Pentecost–the whole of the period from that until His final return is 'the last time.' You will find that sort of distinction in the Old Testament; they talk about the present age and the age to come; the age of the Messiah; the present time and the last times. And here in the New Testament, these different Apostles tell us that now they were already in the last time. John, you notice, says that at the end of the eighteenth verse–'it is the last time'–so that whatever else we may say, it must include that. 'The last time' is sometimes used to cover the whole era, the whole epoch, that lies from the finished work of Christ until His ultimate return in glory.

But it is equally clear that it is not confined to that. Sometimes this phrase 'the last time' is used about certain special epochs. There are times of particular crises and of special judgment, and those times are in a special manner 'the last time.' In other words, as you see in the Old Testament many judgments upon the world, and upon Israel in particular, that prophesy the final judgment, so you see these times that indicate the final last time. So the whole age is the last time; but peculiar eras and epochs when sin and evil are being unusually severe and fierce, and then the time just before the final return of our Lord and Saviour Jesus Christ into this world, that is, as it were, the ultimate last time.

So there have been intervening periods and epochs in the history of the Church, like the terrible persecution of the first Christians, first by the Jews and then by the Roman power and empire. Then there was the terrible period of the dark Middle Ages, and there have been other equally bad times. And the right way, it seems to me, to look at this whole matter is to realise that from the very institution of the Christian Church there has always been this conflict, this mystery of evil, this 'mystery of iniquity' as Paul called it in 2 Thessalonians 2:7, that has been going on right through. There are times when it is unusually fierce and unusually severe and the Church is subjected to particularly terrible trial, but it will all head up to a final conflict of almost staggering dimensions, which will be the immediate prelude to the actual visible return in glory of our Lord and Saviour.

So that, I think, is what John means here by 'the last time,' and that, in turn, brings us to the next term he employs and that is "*the antichrist*," which is a term that is actually only used by the Apostle John. It is very clear that the other writers in different places are concerned about exactly the same thing. Second Thessalonians 2, again, is clearly a description of the same person, the same power, and the same condition. Then in Daniel 7–11 you will find clear descriptions of the same thing, and of course there is another classic passage in Revelation 13 where you get an account of the two beasts, the one arising out of the sea and the other, arising out of the earth. All these are clearly references to the same power, and you get, as it were, incidental references also in 1 Timothy 4 and in 2 Peter 2 and 3.

Now what exactly does John mean by this? He talks about 'antichrist' and says that there are many antichrists who are already in the world at his time. Yet these other teachings lead us very clearly to see that there is something which is also future about the antichrist of which these writers speak. This is a notoriously difficult matter; the literature on the subject is almost endless, and it is extremely difficult to find any consensus of opinion or any general agreement as to what exactly is meant.

These matters of prophecy are very difficult, and people who speak dogmatically about them are just displaying their own ignorance. It is a matter with which the greatest men in the Christian

Church have wrestled from the very beginning, and yet we all know that there are certain pamphlets which seem to be able to explain it quite simply. They only know one view, they have obviously never heard of another, and the whole thing is simple and plain! Well, we know that history has often proved the ignorance and also the error of this oversimplification, and we must approach a matter like this with humility, with caution, and with reverence, knowing that when saintly, godly, able men have confessed the difficulty, it is clearly not something upon which we can easily and glibly pronounce a final judgment.

So let us just look very briefly at some of the views that have been held on this matter.

In the period that followed the Apostle, the view was held by the Church that this was a reference to a Jew who was to arise; that the Temple of Jerusalem would be rebuilt and that this Jew, possessing extraordinary powers and making extraordinary claims, would therefore manifest himself in Jerusalem and would harass and persecute the Christian Church and mislead many Christian people.

That was followed by a phase which can be described more or less as the common teaching of the Roman Catholic Church in the Middle Ages. According to this teaching the antichrist was finally to be a great worldly power–not a Jew of necessity, but a great earthly power and potentate who would establish himself with great claims and who with his great material power would tyrannise the Church, but would finally be destroyed at the coming of Christ. This was the view of the Middle Ages, and it is still more or less the Roman Catholic view.

Then we come to the view of the Protestant Reformation. Speaking in general, the Protestant Reformers were perfectly convinced in their minds that the antichrist was none other than the Roman Catholic Church herself, and especially the Pope. They said that it is clear that this power arises from within the body of the church, hence the term *anti*christ–not so much opposed to Christ as trying to take the place of Christ and opposing Him in that subtle manner. Paul says that this will happen in the Temple and that he will reveal great signs and wonders. There is all this evidence, they said, that the antichrist comes out of the true Church; so they believed that the antichrist is the Roman Catholic Church, and particularly the Pope and the whole power of the papacy.

These have been the leading views that have been held throughout the centuries. Now what is it that we can find about this antichrist in order that we may look at these views and try to evaluate them? We can say this much: the antichrist is one who, in one sense, stands instead of Christ, taking the Christian name and yet opposing the very kingdom of truth which the name implies. John says, 'As ye have heard that antichrist shall come, even now are there many antichrists. . . . They went out from us, but they were not of us; for if they had been of us, they would no doubt have continued with us: but they went out, that they might be made manifest that they were not all of us.' So that when we think of the antichrist, we have to bear that in mind. 'These antichrists who have arisen,' says John, 'belonged to us, but they were not of us.' In other words, they took up the Christian position, they claimed they were Christian, they professed to be teachers of the Christian Church, and yet they have been separated from the Christians in order that it would be clear to all that they were not of them. In other words, they claimed to delight in the true religion and yet they destroyed it.

At the same time it is clear there were many theories of the ultimate mystery which is going to be revealed, the mystery of iniquity. Already they appear, says the Apostle Paul, and yet this man is to come. Now all these things we can put perfectly clearly. The antichrist, or the antichrists, are the various teachers of the gospel who, while they profess to believe the gospel, pervert its teaching in such a way as finally to destroy it. Again you see why the Reformers thought of that aspect of the papal power which called itself the 'representative of Christ,' the great one who really could forgive sins. That is the kind of argument the Reformers used, and you remember how Paul in Acts 20 warned the people of Ephesus that these various teachers would arise amongst them and would, in this very subtle way and manner, mislead and entice many away from the truth.

So to summarise the teaching with regard to this subject, it seems to me that there are things of which we can be certain, though a great deal remains uncertain. The antichrist was already at work in the days of Paul and of John. Secondly, it is abundantly clear that although there have been many imitations of him, he will reach his maximum power just before the end of this age. I think it is equally clear that Daniel pictures the political aspect of this power, whereas Paul emphasises the ecclesiastical aspect, and in Revelation 13 you get both–the beast from the sea (the political), the beast from the earth (the ecclesiastical). Indeed we cannot be certain but that these two aspects might very well follow one another instead of coming together. First a terrible political power and then a terrible ecclesiastical power–a great deal can be said for that view. And the last point, I think, of which we can be certain is that this power will ultimately be concentrated in one particular person. John says there were many antichrists, and yet the teaching is clear that there is going to be an ultimate antichrist, one person, a person having terrible power, able to work miracles and do such wonders that he almost deceives the elect themselves.

Now this, it seems to me, is the very essence of this teaching, and what we have to realise is that in this present age in which we live we are confronted by such a power. Now, of course, the danger at this stage is to be guilty of oversimplification, but what we can be sure of is that from the commencement of the Church until today and from today until the very end there is an evil power at work in the Church. 'We wrestle not against flesh and blood, but against principalities, against powers . . . against spiritual wickedness in high places' (Eph 6:12). John says here that these people have already been warned–'*As ye have heard* that antichrist shall come. . . .' Not one of these Apostles seems to have preached without warning the people against this danger, and yet how ignorant we often are of it.

So the Church is always confronted by this subtle power, a seducing power, a power that represents itself in the name of Christ and yet is denying Christ, for that, you observe, is the very essence of this false teaching. He is 'a liar,' says John 'that denieth that Jesus is the Christ. He is antichrist, that denieth the Father and the Son.'

So the particular characteristic teaching of this antichrist who opposes us, not always openly but often in a very subtle manner, is that he denies that Jesus is the Christ.

Now I reminded you, when we began to deal with this epistle,[1] that no doubt John had in his mind in a very special way these denials of Jesus as Christ. There were two main manifestations of that. There were those who said that Jesus was only a man and that was the end of it, He was just a great teacher and nothing more. But as we have considered, there was also that subtle Gnostic error which said that the eternal Christ had come upon Jesus at His baptism and had left Him on the cross. So that Jesus the Son of God never died; it was the man Jesus who died–Christ had left him before death. They talked about Jesus, but they denied that He is the Christ.

But the Christian teaching is that Jesus Christ is God-man, and the God-man died and did the work, and any denial of that is a manifestation of this antichrist. So a denial of the deity of Christ is a manifestation of the antichrist. Yes, but a denial of the humanity is equally a manifestation of antichrist! There were some who taught that Christ had a phantom body, which was why John said in his Gospel, 'The Word was made flesh, and dwelt among us' (John 1:14); that is why he tells us we have 'seen' and 'handled' Him (1 John 1:1)–the reality of the Incarnation. It was not a phantom body but a true body; the Son of God died literally and actually, and He rose again.

Now this is not only a subtle but also a difficult subject. The great thing for us to realise is that this tendency thus to deny that Jesus is the Christ has been running through the whole long history of the Church; and what light this casts upon the history of the Church! If you read the accounts of the Christian Church in those first centuries, you will find that they talked about the nature of Christ–the two natures but one person. The Greek philosophers came into the Church and said, 'Yes, we believe Jesus Christ but not that explanation of His person.' So the Christian Church had to fight for her life on this very doctrine in those first centuries.

Then you find it in the dark Middle Ages in the domination of the Roman Catholic Church with its priesthood–those intermediaries between man and God; all that is a denial that Jesus is the Christ. And then look back across the Protestant story, especially of the last hundred years, with the subtle denial by the Church herself that Jesus is the Christ, the denial of the miraculous and the supernatural, the idea that Jesus is a great teacher perhaps, a political teacher or a great moral example, but not the Christ. All these are but manifestations of these antichrists, of the ultimate great antichrist who is to come; and our business is to relate all these to our own day and time and to our own generation.

We are living in the last time in that general sense. We may be living in a last time also in a more particular sense. Not only Christians, but also many secular writers and historians at the present time are teaching us that we are living in what they call an 'age of transition,' in one of the great turning-points of history and there can be no doubt but that this is perfectly true. We are living in a time when essential changes are taking place in the history of mankind; there has been no such period at any rate since the Renaissance or the Protestant Reformation.

It is one of those turning-points when things which appeared to be stable are being shaken; there can be no doubt at all but that Western civilisation is coming to an end. It is certainly one of the last times, and there are those who tell us it is *the* last time. I am not prepared to argue with them; my own personal position is that I am not convinced. I would not like to say whether they are right or wrong. I know that many times before, people have said that it was the last time, but it was not so. Every age is liable to think that it is the last time; every period of trial and of difficulty and turmoil in the Church and world tends to make people say, 'This is the end.' So let us be careful.

But what we can be certain of is that the power of iniquity is working. He was working in the time of Paul, and he is working in a very special manner today. It is a time of judgment; it is the time when God's people must be very careful and very circumspect, when they must be doubly certain of the truth and their position. They must beware of this subtle power that would lead them astray, and they must learn to stand, as John exhorts, valiantly for the truth.

May God give us grace to consider, to read about, and to think about these things again, that we may be forewarned and therefore forearmed.

*9*

# Of the Church

> Little children, it is the last time: and as ye have heard that antichrist shall come, even now are there many antichrists; whereby we know that it is the last time. They went out from us, but they were not of us; for if they had been of us, they would no doubt have continued with us: but they went out, that they might be made manifest that they were not all of us.
>
> 1 JOHN 2:18-19

John, let me remind you, introduces us here to the whole question of the spiritual conflict, this great theme of the entire New Testament. As Christian people, as soon as we come into the Christian life we become part of this mighty conflict between the forces of God and the forces of hell, and we are involved in it whether we like it or not. So what he does here is to try to enlighten these people with regard to that; he warns and prepares them to meet and withstand it. We saw that we can divide this section up into three parts: first of all, the importance of realising not only that we are in the conflict but also the nature of that conflict; secondly, the equipment that has been given us to enable us to meet and combat it; and thirdly, the appeal and the exhortation, or, if you like, the reasons which John adduces and gives us for our resistance to this malign power, and for our maintaining the good fight of faith.

Now we have begun our consideration of the first. We have

looked at the doctrine of the antichrist and at what is meant by 'the last time,' and I have drawn some general lessons from that. But we cannot leave it at that. The very words of these two phrases tell us to go on and apply it still further. John here puts this particular doctrine of the 'antichrist' and 'the last time' in terms of the Christian Church herself, and we must consider what he has to say about that because that, in a sense, is the most urgent matter which confronts us as individual Christians and as members of the Christian Church at this present hour.

Let me put it like this: We are all aware of the fact that we are living in a very difficult and critical period; there has been a great falling away in the Christian Church. Compare churches and attendances at churches today with what it was earlier this century. Then it was the thing to do and the custom to go to God's house on Sunday; the Church was popular, and the Church counted. But now it is almost an exception to be a member of a Christian church, and because of that, certain things are tending to happen. Because of this dwindling in the Christian Church, because also of the attacks that are being made on the Church from the outside–the attack on civilisation, the materialistic politics and all these other things–because of this present grave situation, certain things tend to happen to many who are within the Church.

It seems to me, further, that it is essential that we should face together what the Apostle has to say, because at this point his words are as relevant to us now as they were in the first century when he wrote them. There are very many whose faith is being shaken because of the present position. There is a kind of encouragement, after all, in proving that we are only natural and human, and there are many people who look at the dwindling Church and the dwindling attendance and are liable and tempted to ask, 'I wonder if this is right after all? Are we, who are but a handful of people, the only ones who are right, and are the masses, the great majority of people, wrong?' The time of falling away is always a time when people's faith is under attack. We all tend to conform to 'the thing to do.' We follow the majority, and there are many who are filled with a sense of foreboding and who find that their faith is being seriously shaken. In other words, there is a good deal of despondency and pessimism.

Indeed, if I were asked to name the peculiar temptation that confronts us as Christians in these days, I would say it is the tendency to despair, the tendency to become profoundly pessimistic. As we look at the situation, we are tempted to say, 'What of the future? How can the Church possibly go on?' Now that is the kind of condition with which John deals, because of course such despondency leads to confusion. A time of difficulty not only leads to despair–it is also a time in which there is a tendency to panic. People become frantic and desperate and say, 'We must do something to save the Christian Church.' They look at the numbers; they emphasise statistics; they say, 'We must be up and doing–we must organise something to stop the rot.' And so they rush into a busy activity.

So it behooves us to consider the message that the Apostle has for people in that precise situation–what has he to say? Let me try to summarise the message by putting it in the form of some three or four propositions.

The first thing John tells us is that we must not be surprised or alarmed at such a situation. 'Little children,' he says, 'it is the last time: and as ye have heard that antichrist shall come, even now are there many antichrists.' 'You have heard that it is coming,' says John, and that is the first point which we must emphasise. It seems to me that there is nothing, in a sense, which so thoroughly tests our knowledge of the New Testament Scripture, indeed of the whole Bible, there is nothing which so certainly tests our faith as our reaction to the situation in which we find ourselves. If we are given to panic or a sense of despair, it is because we have not read our Scriptures truly, for the Bible is literally full of warnings of the very kind of thing which we are experiencing. Those who know their Bible should not be surprised at the state of the world as it is, nor at the state of the Church. There is nothing at all which is so false and so far removed from the New Testament picture of the Church as the idea that the Church of God, from the beginning, should go on to develop and increase, so that every century should see the Church stronger than she was before, and that this should go on until you arrive at a state when the whole world has become

Christian. There is no passage anywhere in the Scriptures to support such a view.

Indeed, I have tried to show that it is the exact opposite. Read the epistles in the New Testament, go back even before that to the book of the Acts of the Apostles, and you will find that the first preachers of the gospel warned the first believers. They said, 'You are going into a fight, a conflict. There is a mighty, subtle adversary opposed to us, and he will fight to ruin and destroy the Church.' All the prophecies–about the man of sin, the antichrist and so on–are here before us. Indeed, you remember, our blessed Lord Himself asked this question: 'When the Son of Man cometh, shall he find faith on the earth?' (Luke 18:8). No, this idea that the Church was going to be an institution which would increase and ever go onwards and upwards is not based upon Scripture but upon a false philosophy, a false teaching.

Now I do not hesitate to assert that the very state of the Church and of the world is one of the most striking and amazing confirmations of Scriptural teaching that one can ever find. We must, therefore, not be surprised; we must not be amazed or shaken. There is a sense, though it may sound paradoxical, in which the weakness of the Church today should confirm our faith and be an assurance to us of the truth of the Word of God. So, far from being cast down, we should, in a sense, be able to say as we confront the present situation, 'The very wrath of man shall praise Thee, and is praising Thee.' Man, in spite of himself, is confirming the word of God.

The second principle is this: the Church's first consideration at a time like this should be the purity of her doctrine. I think that follows obviously. You remember what John says. 'Little children, this is the last time: and as ye have heard that antichrist shall come, even now are there many antichrists, whereby we know that it is the last time. They went out from us, but they were not of us; for if they had been of us, they would no doubt have continued with us: but they went out, that they might be made manifest that they were not all of us.'

In other words, John's great concern in this whole section is not at all about the numbers in the Church, about the fact that so many had left, but rather about the purity of the doctrine of the Church. These antichrists were the people who denied that Jesus is the Christ; they denied the Son and the Father; they denied the Trinity. So as you read these words, indeed this entire section of the whole epistle, you will find the one thing that John is concerned about is the true doctrine.

Let me emphasise this because, surely, it is a point that needs to be emphasised at the present time. John, I say, is not interested in numbers, nor is he interested in organisation. Is this not one of the subtle temptations that comes to us today? So much of our talk and interest centres upon numbers and the organisation. This is very natural, very human; we like facts and figures and statistics. We, because we are the inheritors of certain traditions, tend to think of the Christian Church in a building and as a gathering of people, a denomination, or as an interdenominational organisation. We were brought up to think of the Church in some such terms, and our whole thinking tends to be controlled by such mechanical statistics.

But my point is that as you read the New Testament you will find that idea to be false to the very atmosphere of the New Testament. The great thing that is emphasised here is the purity of the Church and not her size. I wonder whether we are prepared to face the fact that the Church of God in this age and generation may in a sense have to go back to the catacombs. We may have to face that; there are people who are facing that, and it is the position in many countries today. The Church is 'in the home of so and so,' as it was in the New Testament, and we must realise that the Church is quite as much the Church if she is a handful of people as if she is a great crowd; the thing that matters in the Church is not numbers, not organisation, it is the purity of the doctrine.

We can see the relevance of this to the present position. You read constantly in the religious books and journals, and even in the newspapers, an argument which works itself out like this: They say that the Christian Church today is fighting for her life; there are forces and factors in the world inimical to her and opposed to the doctrine of the gospel. We see these mighty forces, organised and amalgamated, and there they are facing the Church. We see our own dwindling numbers and congregations, and the statistics are telling their tale from year to year. So what are we to do? They say, 'There is only one thing to do; we must all get together. This is no time for arguing about what people may believe; if they believe in God and use the name Christian they are one with us. So let's all get together and form a union to face this common enemy.'

Now obviously there is a sense in which we are all in a kind of general sympathy with such talk, and yet it seems to me that unless we are careful we shall be denying one of the essential New Testament doctrines. I say that whatever the feeling may be, whatever the departure from the Church, the one thing we should be concerned about is the purity of the doctrine. Better a handful of people who believe that Jesus is the Christ than a crowd who are uncertain as to whether He is or not and who falsely use the word 'Christian.' 'These people,' says John, 'have gone out from you in a sense; but,' he goes on to say, 'that does not matter; the question is, are you who remain all right?' The purity of doctrine is paramount: *Jesus is the Christ.*

In other words, we must realise that true unity can only be obtained in terms of truth. Yes, you can have your unions, you can have your amalgamations, you can have your coalitions apart from truth; but it is impossible to have the unity of the Spirit except in terms of truth. The Holy Spirit binds people together who are agreed about the doctrine–people who say, 'Jesus is the Lord' and who recognise Him as the unique Son of God–people who believe in the Incarnation, in the atoning sacrifice, in the Resurrection, and in the person of the Holy Spirit–that is the doctrine without which there can be no real union.

Now that is the doctrine of the whole Bible. Have you not noticed how in a most ironical manner and almost with an element, if one may use the word, of divine humour the Bible pours its sarcasm upon great numbers? Is there any doctrine in the Bible from beginning to end like the doctrine of the remnant? Is there anything that stands out so much as that God has done everything through one man who stood in the breach alone? Go through the Scriptures and see how God often deliberately reduced the numbers. Read the story of Gideon and see how he gets rid of a great crowd until he has only a handful left. Yes, they are the people who come to realise that their doctrine is pure and that this God can vanquish the mighty enemy. This is the doctrine of the Scriptures. It is the power of the Spirit that matters. We have a power behind us and in us which is mightier than the enemy and which must prevail, but He only honours those who honour Him; He only recognises those who profess and confess the pure doctrine.

The Apostle Paul said exactly the same as John says here. There were many leaving the Church at the time, and poor Timothy had become depressed. He could see the people going away and following false teaching, believing those who said that the resurrection was past already. He had been sending his mournful notes to Paul, and Paul's reply was, 'The foundation of God standeth sure' (2 Tim 2:19). God knows those who are His; it is the purity of the faith and of the doctrine that matters.

But that in turn, I think, brings us to the next point. Having thus seen that the present position must not depress us, having seen that it is the purity of doctrine that matters, the next thing to do is to examine ourselves. 'Little children, it is the last time . . . they went out from us,' and the question is, what about us? John here plainly teaches us something like this: The mere fact that we claim we are Christians and that we belong to the Church does not prove that we are Christians. 'They went out from us, they were amongst us,' these antichrists whom he is denouncing and the people who believed they were within the Christian Church. 'These people had joined the Church, they had claimed to be Christians, yet,' says John, 'they have gone out from us, proving they were not of us though they had been amongst us.'

Now, it seems to me that this is a serious and important thing for us. That may sound a rather surprising and startling thing to say, and there are people who would say that you should not be pressing an examination like that at the present time. 'The churches are small enough as it is,' they say; 'are you going to tell people to examine themselves and cause a still greater drift? Surely, you should rather encourage the people to come in!' But the New Testament does not do that; it has never done so. Rather it says that it is possible for people to be in the Christian Church and yet not be of her.

Let me put it like this–and I do so by way of encouragement and comfort. We may think, as we look at the modern Church, and as we compare and contrast it with what appertained earlier this century, that we have fallen upon evil days and that the Church is no longer the Church of God. But look at it like this: at one time everybody went to church, and the churches were packed and crowded. But are we to assume from that that everybody who went to church was a true Christian? There were people who went to church for very strange and curious reasons; it was a habit or a custom; it was a social thing; it paid for people to go to church. No, we must not assume that because the churches were packed they were packed with Christians; here were people who were in the Church, and yet they were all wrong. So it behooves us to examine ourselves and to make certain that we are truly of the faith and truly in Christ.

The ultimate test is that we are *of* the Church. That is how John puts it–'they went out from us, but they were not of us; for if they had been of us, they would no doubt have continued with us.' What does this mean exactly; how may I know whether I am really of the Church or not? Well, it surely means this: True Christians are those who are in vital union with the Church. They are not loosely attached to it; they have not just got their names on the roll. They do not merely recognise a general sort of allegiance once a day or on some special Sunday. No, they are bound by vital bonds of union. In other words, they have life in them; they do not have to force themselves, but rather, they cannot help themselves. It is the difference between a member of the family and a great friend of the family; there is something within that tells them, 'This is my life; I am bound to them; these are my people.' For them it is the big thing; they are bound by bonds of life itself; it is an organic and vital union, and the result is that they are in true fellowship with other Christians. They feel bound to them in a sense that they are not bound to anybody else. They feel that they understand them in a way that they do not understand anybody else; they feel that the Church is their home in a sense that nothing else is their home–'*of* us.'

There, it seems to me, is the vital distinction. So we ask ourselves a simple question: where do these things come in my daily life? What exactly is the place and value of these things in my experience? What is my attitude towards the whole thing? Is it central and vital, or is it something on the periphery of which I constantly have to remind myself? The people who are not 'of us' are the people who are on the fringe, and when anything goes wrong they are always the first to go away.

And that brings me to the last principle: We must, according to John, try to see the place and purpose of a time like this in the plan of God; how do we relate it all to God's great purpose? And John answers that question like this:

God, according to John, had in a sense thrust these people out of the Church in order that a distinction might be made, in order that He might show the false and reveal and manifest the true. Now I interpret that in this way: A time like this is one of great value to the Christian Church; it is a time that tests us. So we take courage, then, Christian friends, as we remind ourselves of this. The 'thing to do' in the modern world is not to worship God, is not to go to a place of worship; indeed, there seems to be every reason and excuse for not doing so, and the fact that we are concerned about these things in and of itself proclaims a great deal concerning us. A time like this tests people, and those who hold on to these things at such a time have got something. The majority are not interested, and how easy it is to go with them!

There is a sense in which we should glory in the fact that we are here today and not in the later Victorian era. Then everybody would have been going to church so we would not have been tested. But now we are being tested; we are being sifted and examined; we are reading literature that is opposed to us; we see the crowd going the other way, and still we stand. Paul was saying that same thing in his letter to Timothy. John the Baptist said the same thing about our Lord: 'whose fan is in his hand, and he will thoroughly purge his floor, and gather his wheat into the garner; but he will burn up the chaff with unquenchable fire' (Matt 3:12). It is a time of sifting the wheat and the chaff. A time like this obviously gets rid of that which is wrong and false and thereby cleanses the Church. The loose adherents leave, the people with the doubtful doctrine go, and thereby the dead branches are being removed and the Church is being cleansed and purged and purified.

Here again is a doctrine running right through Scripture. You find it at all times of revival; indeed, to me one of the most striking things during the period of revival is the idea of discipline. We read in the *Journals* of John Wesley about how he insisted on church discipline. They made a fair show of numbers and then he proceeded to examine the church. He invited the members one by one, and he adds a kind of laconic note at the end of his account in which he says that when he had finished they were below three hundred! It is this idea of sifting, pruning, getting rid of the dead leaves and branches so that the Church may be purified and cleansed. And the very time in which we are living is doing that. People with false doctrine are disturbed, so many have turned their backs upon them because they have gone astray in their doctrine; and that is helping to purify and cleanse the Church.

But, lastly, a time like this, it seems to me, provides us with a very great ground of assurance, and it does so like this: 'They went out from us,' says John, 'but they were not of us; for if they had been of us, they would no doubt have continued with us.' The Authorised translation here puts in the words 'no doubt,' and in a sense it does help us to understand the meaning–'for if they had been of us, they would no doubt have continued with us'–they have not continued with us, yet we are continuing. Why is that? And there is only one answer finally, and that is that we continue because we must be of the faith.

This, in a sense, is the doctrine of the final perseverance of the saints: 'If they had been of us, they would no doubt have continued with us,' whereas they have been removed. When the false has been taken away, the true remains; those who belong to the Church and are *of* the Church remain steadfast and continue–'the foundation of God standeth sure. . . . The Lord knoweth them that are his' (2 Tim 2:19). And 'neither shall any man pluck them out of my Father's hand' (John 10:28). They will be true, they will be sifted and tested, but if they are of Him they can never be removed.

So we should look at a time like this in that way. It is a time of apostasy, of falling away; it is a time when the faith of many is failing. But we are not seeing the end of the Christian Church. No, the end of the Church will be going to glory; the Church is indestructible. The Church belongs to Him, and all that belong to Him truly are members of His glorious, glorified Body. Therefore, in this remarkable and amazing way there is a sense in which we should glory in the fact that we are in the world at this hour and in the Church at this present difficult time.

Do not misunderstand me. We all mourn the fact that so many are outside Christ; we mourn the fact that the Christian Church is apparently so weak and helpless. Yet we must not covet crowds and numbers; we must be concerned about the purity of the doctrine, the purity of the Church herself in life as well as in her doctrine. We should glory in the fact that at a time of apostasy and falling away we belong to the remnant, and we should look with the eye of faith to the crowning day that is coming, to the day of the return of the Lord with all the hosts of His people, when, though now few in number, we shall belong to that great multitude which no man can number–

*Ten thousand times ten thousand*
*In sparkling raiment bright*
*The armies of the ransomed saints*
*Throng up the steeps of light.*

Henry Alford

We shall be with them. Though small and despised perhaps today, if we are of Him we shall certainly share in the glory that is to come.

*10*

# The Anointing of the Holy Spirit

But ye have an unction from the Holy One, and ye know all things. I have not written unto you because ye know not the truth, but because ye know it, and that no lie is of the truth. . . . But the anointing which ye have received of him abideth in you, and ye need not that any man teach you: but as the same anointing teacheth you of all things, and is truth, and is no lie, and even as it hath taught you, ye shall abide in him.

1 JOHN 2:20-21, 27

In order to have the right setting for these three verses let me briefly remind you again of what the Apostle is doing in this particular section. He is dealing especially in this chapter with the hindrances to a true fellowship with God. There are certain things, in other words, which we must always bear in mind very clearly if we are to continue to enjoy this fellowship with the Father and with His Son, Jesus Christ. This is the greatest blessing of all that the Christian gospel has to offer; greater than forgiveness, greater than peace and joy and all the various sensations which we may know from time to time, is this wonderful fact of fellowship with God the Father and God the Son through the Holy Spirit. Now we have been considering the things that we have to bear in mind which might hinder the fellowship, and so far the Apostle has dealt with what we may describe as the peculiar difficulties that arise as it were with in the Christian life itself.

But here in this section, you remember, from verses 18 to 28 he deals with the difficulty which is a little more external, the difficulty that tends to come to Christian people from outside themselves, but well within the realm of the Christian Church. It is the danger of apostasy, the danger of false doctrine, and that is the great theme of this section: these antichrists who have already come, as John says; and the fact that we are in the last time and that there is a great conflict between mighty spiritual forces going on around and about us. It is the danger of being side-tracked from the truth, the danger of being seduced, as he puts it, into a false view of the Lord Jesus Christ. So that is the theme, and I have suggested that the best way of dividing it is to divide it into three sections–the first of which is to realise the importance of the fact that there is this spiritual conflict going on, because if we do not realise that, then inevitably we shall succumb to it, and we have considered that in its various aspects.

So now we move on to the second section, in which John tells us that provision has been made for us to prevent our going wrong and going astray in that way. And that is the matter which we shall now consider in terms of these three verses. John is writing to people who are still in the Church. As we have seen, some had left, though they had been a part of the Church. 'Now,' says John in effect to the others, 'you remain, you are all right, you have not been seduced by these antichrists. So why do you stay, what is the difference, what is it that has enabled you to reject that false teaching and to stand firm?' And in these three verses he provides us with the answer to those questions.

This is a most important statement, a very vital part of Christian doctrine and one of the most glorious aspects of Christian truth. What is it that enables us to stand and to remain and to avoid the seduction of false teaching which would separate us from God and Christ and eventually take us out and lead to our condemnation? Well, John says here that it is all due to the work of the Holy Spirit. Christians are who they are because of the Holy Spirit.

Christians, he says, are those who have received unction, or *the anointing*–that is his way of describing the Holy Spirit. It is because of Him that they are able to discern and understand and avoid these subtle dangers that threaten them within the realm even of the Christian Church itself. John says in verses 20 and 21, 'But ye have an unction from the Holy One, and ye know all things. I have not written unto you because ye know not the truth, but because ye know it, and that no lie is of the truth.' Then he adds in verse 27, 'But the anointing which ye have received of him abideth in you.'

Now let us, before we go any further, try to get these terms clear. John's words 'unction' or 'anointing' are just a very graphic way of describing the influence and the effect of the Holy Spirit upon the believer. It is the wording of the Old Testament where we are frequently told that prophets, priests and kings, when they were inducted, as it were, were anointed with oil; that was the mechanism, the ceremonial, that was used to set them apart for their office. Samuel anointed first Saul and then David as king; the same anointing was given to the priests and prophets, and the results of that pouring of the oil upon them was that in that way they were regarded as consecrated; they had become anointed ones who were now enabled to do their duty.

Very often you find that the Holy Spirit is compared to oil. The oil that went into the golden candlesticks in the Temple was an illustration of the same thing–the oil that provides the life or the power for the light. Those are the symbols that are used constantly in Scripture for the influence and the power of the Holy Spirit, so that what John is really saying is that every Christian in that sense is one who has been anointed, set apart, by God, and enabled by God to do certain things. If you go through the New Testament you will find that Christians are described as prophets, priests and kings. We are 'a royal priesthood, a holy nation,' says Peter (1 Pet 2:9); and in Revelation we read that we are 'kings and priests unto God' (Rev 1:6); those are the terms that are used. So there is a sense in which it is true to say that as the Lord Jesus Christ is prophet, priest and King as the result of His anointing, so all of us who are Christ's are prophets, priests and kings.

Again, just to complete this picture, we are told that our Lord was, as it were, anointed and set apart for His Messianic and saving work when the Holy Spirit came upon Him in Jordan when He was baptised by John the Baptist; and in that kind of sense, the same thing is true of the individual Christian. 'Ye have an unction from the Holy One,' says John. Who is that? The context makes it quite plain–He is none other than our Lord Himself; and in verse 27 the reference is still to the Lord Jesus Christ.

This is an interesting point which can be looked at in two ways. We are told by the Apostle Paul in Ephesians 4:8 that 'when he ascended up on high he . . . gave gifts unto men.' It was the Lord Jesus Christ who sent the Holy Spirit upon the infant Christian Church. The Holy Spirit did not come until He had ascended up into heaven; then He came. He comes from the Father and the Son, or from the Father through the Son; it is as a result of the perfect work of the Son that the Father gives the Holy Spirit to all who belong to Him. That is one way of looking at it.

But there is another way of looking at it. Because we are incorporated into Christ, and into the life of Christ, we partake of what is true of Him. Therefore, as He has been anointed and has received the Holy Spirit without measure, all of us who are in Him receive the gift of the Holy Spirit because we are in Him. That is why any kind of teaching which would ever suggest to us that you can be a Christian without receiving the Holy Spirit is unscriptural. It is impossible for one to be a Christian and then later on receive the Holy Spirit. To be in Christ means that you are receiving the Spirit; no one can be a Christian in any sense without having already received this unction, this anointing, the gift of the Holy Spirit.

That, then, is what you may like to term the mechanics of the terminology which is employed by the Apostle. But what I want us to consider is the result of all this. There are these people who have remained true in the Church, and they have remained true because they have this unction. So what does this gift of the Spirit lead to? John says here that these Christians 'know all things'–'Ye have an unction from the Holy One, and ye know all things.' Now it is true that another translation is possible at that point; we might read it like this: 'Ye have an unction from the Holy One, and ye all know'–as if to say, 'These people who had come out did not know, but you know because you have an unction.' You can take it either way; both are perfectly legitimate translations.

And then in verse 27 he says, 'But the anointing which ye have received of him abideth in you and ye need not that any man teach you.' These are the main results, according to the Apostle, of receiving this anointing of the Holy Spirit, and the question at once arises, What does this mean? I need scarcely remind you that this is a very important and vital doctrine. These two verses have been the debating ground of people within the Christian Church from the very beginning, so let me just give you a few historical details about these verses and the doctrine contained in them.

They were in a very special manner the great theme of the dispute in the seventeenth century between the Puritans and the Quakers. It is a most fascinating study just to read something of the history of that century and of the church in this country at that time. In the Puritan movement you find the gradual development of an extreme radical wing which eventually became the Quakers. There are a number of books on this subject, one of which is called *The Holy Spirit in Puritan Thought and Practice* by Nuttall. I strongly recommend it to those who are interested in this matter. The great point at issue was this: what exactly is the relationship between the Holy Spirit in the Christian and the Word of God?

That was the dispute between the Puritans and the Quakers. The Quakers tended to emphasise what they called the 'inner light'–this unction, and they tended to say that that was sufficient, that they received a direct revelation, that the Word of God was unnecessary and that in a sense they were inspired as were the first apostles. That was not true of all Quakers, but it was certainly true of some of them. 'We are told by John,' they said, 'that we have an unction from the Holy One; we know all things, and we need not that any man should teach us. We have this inner light, this inner monitor, this enlightening, and we do not need any instruction; we do not need to be guided by the Word of God.'

But this is not only something that emerges in the history of the Puritans and the Quakers; it is a question that is always raised by the whole teaching of mysticism. Mystics tend to look inwards; they believe that God is resident within them and that really the way to be blessed of God and to live the spiritual life in the full sense is to look within, to dwell within, and to be sensitive to the vision that speaks to you and the light that is given you and the leading and the guidance. It is the inward process, the turning inward on oneself, the belief that God is in the depths of one's being. So the idea of mysticism always has likewise raised, in a very acute form, the very doctrine that John mentions here; so the mystics are generally fond of these verses which we are considering together.

But the matter also tends to arise in a third way. Whenever a special emphasis is placed upon the Holy Spirit, this problem invariably arises. There are today, as there were very commonly and generally in the history of the Church, certain groups of Christian people who seem to put more emphasis on the teaching concerning the work of the Holy Spirit than anything else. They believe the other doctrines, yes, it is true; but their great emphasis is upon the Holy Spirit, and the moment you tend to do that you tend again to raise in an acute form the doctrine which the Apostle is dealing with in these verses.

So let me try to sum up what I would call the tendencies that almost invariably follow whenever you get this special emphasis upon the Holy Spirit and the subjective aspect of the Christian life. These are the things that tend to follow: The first is that there is almost invariably a claim to direct revelations; such friends always tell us something has 'come to them' or it 'has been shown to' them. In other words, they do not hesitate to claim that as the Holy Spirit taught the Apostle Paul and these other apostles and revealed the truth to them, they too, in a sense, are receiving truth directly and immediately from the Holy Spirit. The seventeenth-century Quakers did not hesitate to claim that, and there are people today who would claim the same thing. They say, 'Because I have the Holy Spirit, I am as inspired as if I were an apostle'–a claim to direct revelation.

The second tendency is to judge everything by means of their subjective state and condition. You will find that certain people use a phrase like this: they say that the way to judge truth is to judge whether or not it produces the 'rising of Christ within'; if it does produce this, then it is true–if it does not, it is false. Truth becomes subjective, the effect it has on me.

Another tendency is this, and it follows, I think, of necessity the tendency to depreciate the place and the importance, the value and the position of the Holy Scriptures in the Christian life and in our own experience. The more you emphasise this subjective state and condition, the less need is there for the objective Word, and that is why you always find the tendency amongst such people to say, 'Ah, these others are mechanical; they are tying it down to "the Word." They haven't had this subjective experience, and they are always talking about something external.' You find that most mystics are not famous for reading the Scriptures regularly; indeed you often find something like this: They say that one verse is enough for them; 'one verse sets me thinking so I begin to think and then things happen to me'; and they get this 'revelation.' They do not read their Scriptures systematically, and that obviously must tend to depreciate it.

And the last tendency is always towards a claim of infallibility. Go back to the history of the Quakers and you find it there. They tended to claim a kind of infallibility for themselves, and if you read the history or study any movement which emphasises the mystical, the inner light, or this principle of inner guidance, you will, I think, without a single exception always find that somewhere or another in such a movement there is either a pope or a number of popes. There is always somebody whose guidance is infallible and who cannot go wrong, and so you find this principle of infallibility reasserting itself.

Those, then, are some of the dangers and tendencies that arise from a misinterpretation of these three verses. So that leads us to the positive question: what then does the Apostle really teach? Well, once more perhaps we must put it negatively before we come to the positive. To start with, before we go any further, let us be quite clear that the Apostle is not dealing with the question of guidance; these verses have nothing at all to do with that. They are not concerned to teach me with regard to this whole difficult question of how I am to know what God wants me to do with regard to particular decisions. John is discussing here a knowledge of truth, a knowledge of doctrine; his concern is the truth of the doctrine that Jesus is the Christ. That is the context, so we must exclude everything else.

Secondly, he does not teach here that every Christian receives fresh truth directly and immediately even as the apostles did, for his whole case, in a sense, is that he has already told these people that he writes to them in order that they may have fellowship with him and with the other apostles. They have received the truth which they have believed through the apostolic witness and teaching and preaching; they are, as it were, the second generation of believers. These people had not received the truth directly by divine illumination. No, the apostles had gone around preaching the Word to them, so that is how they had entered into that fellowship, and the fellowship which the apostles had was fellowship with the Father and with His Son, Jesus Christ.

Or let us look at the way in which the Apostle Paul puts this. Paul, describing the Church in Ephesians 2:20, says that it is established 'upon the foundation of apostles and prophets.' So they are the foundation, and you cannot repeat the foundation–there is only one. You can build upon it and put stones and bricks upon it, but you cannot repeat it; the building is not a succession of foundations. So the claim of the New Testament everywhere is that the apostles and prophets are a separate and unique body of people. It was to them that the Holy Spirit specially revealed this truth that they recorded in these Scriptures and on which we build and by which we must walk and on which our whole faith must rest. The apostles and prophets are a class apart, and therefore for people to claim that they are as uniquely and directly and divinely inspired as the apostles and prophets is to contradict the plain teaching of Scripture. We, as Christians, are not supposed to receive fresh truth. The truth, the faith, has been once and for ever delivered to the saints and to the apostles. We cannot go into this in detail, but you will find that the Roman Catholic Church does not believe that; the Roman Catholic Church says she is as divinely inspired today as were the apostles and prophets. She claims to have received fresh truth since the end of the New Testament canon. The Quakers make the same sort of claim–God has revealed something to them.

They all claim this special revelation. But it is a denial of the plain teaching of the Scriptures.

Thirdly, John does not teach here that a Christian knows everything. 'But surely,' says someone, 'when it says "ye know all things," doesn't "all things" mean just that?' But if you think that, then you must mean that every Christian knows everything–astronomy, geometry, the classics and everything else that is in the realm of knowledge–which is patently and obviously ridiculous! No, we must take these statements within their context. John obviously does not mean secular knowledge.

Does he then mean spiritual knowledge? No, he does not mean spiritual knowledge either, in every sense, for this good reason. If John is here saying that every man or woman who receives the Holy Spirit automatically knows the whole of spiritual truth, how can you apply the New Testament teaching about growing in grace and in knowledge? How can there be any development in our knowledge and understanding? Not only that, I think we can say that if that were true, then there would be no need for the New Testament epistles. Clearly that is not the case. John's reference to 'all things' here is a reference to the particular subject with which he is dealing; it is not an all-inclusive, all-comprehensive statement.

Let us go back again to this question of infallibility. John does not teach here that because of this knowledge every Christian is infallible. We can prove that in this way: If the unction of the Holy Spirit means that every Christian knows everything and is therefore infallible, it would follow of necessity that every Christian would have to agree with every other Christian about every aspect of Christian doctrine. But that is not the case. There are divergences and differences amongst Christians who manifest the Holy Spirit in their lives–about the question of baptism, about the prophetic teaching, about church order and many other subjects. So that automatically, it seems to me, rules out this whole possibility of infallibility. Not only that, Christians–good Christians–have from time to time fallen into error. They have gone astray in their doctrine and have subsequently acknowledged it; so there is no such thing as infallibility here.

And lastly, I would point out that negatively this does not teach that the Christian needs no instruction. 'But surely,' says someone, 'that must be wrong. Does not your text say, "and the anointing which ye have received of him abideth in you, and ye need not that any man teach you"? Surely you are playing with words; you are not being true and honest in your interpretation. John says, we do not need any man to teach us and yet you say that the Christian Church still needs instruction. How do you reconcile this?'

It seems to me that the answer is as simple as this: the very fact that John is writing to them proves that they need instruction. If they do not, then John need have no concern about them at all. If the Christian needs no instruction, then the apostles' claim to be divinely inspired when they wrote their epistles was a sheer waste of time. These epistles are full of instruction. We are told that the Christian is to 'grow in grace, and in the knowledge of our Lord and Saviour Jesus Christ' (2 Pet 3:18); there is milk provided for him, and then there is strong meat. That is impossible if you take this statement literally and maintain that John is saying the Christian never needs any teaching. No, clearly that is not what he means.

So let us put it in this positive form: Surely the context here determines the interpretation. What John is really saying is what the Apostle Paul says in 1 Corinthians 2:13, 14. He is saying that the Christian has spiritual understanding which the natural man has not. These things are only understood in a spiritual manner, and what John is here saying is that the Christian, having received the Holy Spirit, has a spiritual understanding. 'The natural man receiveth not the things of the Spirit of God: for they are foolishness unto him: neither can he know them because they are spiritually discerned,' says Paul, and John says the same thing here. 'You,' says John, 'are holding fast to this truth because the Holy Spirit has given you this enlightenment and understanding.'

What is this truth about? Well, John is dealing here with the particular doctrine of the birth of our Lord–'I have not written unto you because ye know not the truth, but because ye know it, and that no lie is of the truth. Who is a liar but he that denieth that Jesus is the Christ?' (vv 21-22). That is what John means. These people, because they had the Holy Spirit and His enlightenment, understood the doctrine concerning the person of the Lord Jesus Christ and the work that He had come to perform. If they had not received the Spirit, they could not have done that, but they did understand these things. They understood the doctrine of the two natures in one person. They understood the doctrine of the death of Christ upon the Cross; they understood the doctrine of justification by faith; they had an unction which enabled them to explain these things–'we have the mind of Christ,' says Paul (1 Cor 2:16).

This is the wonderful thing that is true of Christians. They may not have much natural ability, but if they have the Holy Spirit they can understand this truth, and that is why the Christian faith is not only a faith for philosophers–it is a faith for anybody. It is not something that depends upon the natural man's ability; it is an enlightenment, an unction. The Holy Spirit enables men and women to see and to understand something of the glorious nature of salvation. Though they may be simple, though they may be ignorant, though the world may dub them as being unintelligent, if they have this enlightenment they understand things that the greatest natural philosopher cannot understand.

That is what John says: 'You understand these things; the other man does not.' Or we can put it like this: because they have this anointing, Christians understand error and are able to save themselves from deviations from the truth. I can put this in historical form. It has often been the case in the Christian Church that when the learned and all the professors have gone astray and became wrong in their doctrine, certain simple people have remained steadfast and solid in the truth. You often find that in the past. When the whole Roman Catholic Church seemed to have gone wrong in its doctrine in so many vital respects, there were those in various parts of the continent of Europe who held to the simplicity of the faith.

That is what John is saying, and there is a sense in which something like this has been happening in the last hundred years. Simple people have heard and recognised the centralities of the faith when the more learned have all become confused and have tended to go astray; it is because of this unction and it is in that sense that the Christian needs no instruction. There is no need to instruct Christians about the person of Christ, for they know it if they are

Christians at all. That is why John says, 'I write unto you because you know the truth–you would not be a Christian if you did not know these things. How can you be a Christian if you are not right about the person of the Lord and about His death and about the Resurrection and so on? I am writing to you because you know them, and I am writing especially to you to point out the kind of subtle seduction that is threatening you.'

The writer of the epistle to the Hebrews put it like this: 'Let us go on unto perfection' (Heb 6:1). 'I do not want,' he says in effect, 'to lay again the foundation, the first principles; you know all these things, because if you do not you are not a Christian at all. I am going on now to deal with these higher principles. You need teaching there because you have only been babes so far; now I am going on to higher doctrine.' Did Paul not say the same thing in writing to the Corinthians: 'We speak wisdom among them that are perfect' (1 Cor 2:6). The Christian does not need instruction about first principles; he already knows them; that is why he is a Christian–that is what John is saying here.

And lastly, he says that if we have this unction and anointing of the Holy Spirit in us, it will keep us in the truth and in the faith. Is there not something wonderful about the history of the Christian Church? The Holy Spirit came upon her on the day of Pentecost, and He has remained in the Church ever since. Yes, there have been times of terrible apostasy, there have been times of falling away, there have been times when the leaders of the Church all seem to have gone wrong, and yet the remnant has always remained. Why? Because the unction of the Holy Spirit abides, keeping them in the faith, keeping them in the truth.

And, thank God, while this unction and anointing abides in us we cannot go wrong. I do not hesitate to make that assertion. Those who are truly God's people cannot go wrong in their doctrine on particular aspects. About the person of Christ and about the way of salvation, on these two vital fundamental things, they cannot go astray–the unction keeps them. They may listen to false teaching about certain other matters which are not vital and central; but about these things which determine whether people are Christians or not, the unction and the anointing of the Holy Spirit will keep them and hold them and sustain them. And while others go out and leave and fall away, these will remain because they see it, and having seen it, they cannot possibly believe anything else.

That is the doctrine. We have been anointed and been set apart; we have received this unction, and it has given us this understanding of truth which enables us to say that 'we have the mind of Christ' (1 Cor 2:16).

# 11

# The Truth and the Lie

Who is a liar but he that denieth that Jesus is the Christ? He is antichrist, that denieth the Father and the Son. Whosoever denieth the Son, the same hath not the Father: but he that acknowledgeth the Son hath the Father also. . . . And this is the promise that he hath promised us, even eternal life. . . . And now, little children, abide in him; that, when he shall appear, we may have confidence, and not be ashamed before him at his coming.

1 JOHN 2:22-23, 25, 28

I take those four verses together because they are the four verses with which we have not already dealt in our consideration of this section which runs from verses 18–28. We have seen that the themes of this section are: the character of the enemy who is opposed to us; the understanding that is given us with respect to him; and then the way in which to fight him, or the arguments which we use in order to stimulate ourselves for the fight in order that we may defeat him. It is that third matter which we are concerned with now in these verses. They, again, are full of interest; indeed, it would be good if we could take the time to deal in detail with each verse separately. Take verse 22: 'Who is a liar but he that denieth that Jesus is the Christ.' The language which is used there by the Apostle is very strong; he does not hesitate to refer to these antichrists as *liars.*

Now that is not only strong language, but it is also, in a sense, somewhat surprising. It comes as a real shock to some people, especially as John has just been previously appealing to us to love the brethren. 'How do you reconcile these two things?' some say. 'Here is the man who appears as the great Apostle of love and who talks so much about love in this particular epistle–so how is it that he should thus describe these people who had gone out, and those who had seduced them, as liars?' This comes as something very strange to many people, especially at the present time, for the great word today is the word *tolerance.* We claim that we are the most tolerant generation that the world has ever known. We do not like strong language and controversy; we rather pride ourselves on having advanced beyond all that in every realm and department. The great thing today is to be getting together and understanding one another's point of view; we should not denounce a point of view as John does here.

There are many instances of this. You have doubtless listened to discussions between Christians and unbelievers on the radio and heard how they often congratulate themselves on being such nice men! They spend so much time in trying to understand one another's point of view. One Christian said recently that we must not hold these views too fiercely and strongly. So certainly we must not call a man who is an unbeliever, and who denies Jesus as the Christ, a liar!

That is, as you will agree, the characteristic of the present mentality and outlook. It is a time for getting together, we are told, and, in view of the common enemy and the unbelief that is facing the Church, we must not be over-punctilious; and if people want to call themselves Christian, then let us welcome it and be glad that they do so, though they may say that Jesus is only a man and not the Son of God. If they are in any way interested in Him and anxious to practise His ethics, let us all get together, even perhaps with those who are just theists and merely believe in the being of God.

That is the modern attitude, and it makes a word like this sound very harsh to our ears. But what we have here is in many ways very characteristic of the New Testament. John is not the exception; John did not use language like this because he was Boanerges, one of 'the sons of thunder' (Mark 3:17)–you find others doing the same thing. Listen to the Apostle Paul using language like that to the Galatians: 'Though we, or an angel from heaven, preach any other gospel unto you than that which we have preached unto you, let him be accursed' (Gal 1:8). You cannot imagine anything stronger than that. Or listen to him as he writes to the Corinthians: 'If any man love not the Lord Jesus Christ, let him be Anathema' (1 Cor 16:22). Again it is very strong language.

Remember, too, the preaching of John the Baptist when he looked at his congregation, which consisted of Pharisees and others, and said, 'O generation of vipers, who hath warned you to flee from the wrath to come?' (Luke 3:7). Think also of the words of our blessed Lord Himself as He addressed the Pharisees, towards the end of His life; He referred to them as 'whited sepulchres' (Matt 23:27). Now I emphasise all this merely because surely we must be rather careful lest we put ourselves into a position in which we claim that we are more Christian than the Lord Jesus Christ Himself and His blessed Apostles. There is a danger that we may confuse sentimentality and a doctrinal laxity and looseness for a true spirit of charity. The New Testament uses the language of which I have just been reminding you, and here it is in its essence–*liars.*

So then, how do we reconcile these things? Well, there is a very real distinction drawn in the New Testament between what we are to endure for ourselves and our response when the truth is attacked. The Sermon on the Mount tells us to 'turn the other cheek'; quite right, there is no inconsistency between what John says here with that teaching. With regard to ourselves and our own personal feelings we are to endure anything and everything; we are not to stand up for ourselves; we are not to call people liars who attack us in person. But where the truth is concerned, where doctrine is involved, where the whole essence of the gospel comes in, and especially the person of the Lord Jesus Christ, we are to stand and be strong and we are not to hesitate to use language like this. As regards ourselves, tolerance and charity; let the world despise us and malign and persecute us and say what it will concerning us–

we are to go steadily forward, expecting such things to happen. But when it becomes a question of truth which is absolutely vital to salvation and to the glory of God, there must be no compromise and there must be no attempt just to accommodate ourselves to the other person's point of view. We are rather to take the position of John and to say, 'Who is a liar but he that denieth that Jesus is the Christ.'

Now this is a very dangerous statement to make. It is very easy to persuade ourselves that we are just manifesting righteous indignation and 'being angry and sinning not' when really we are just contending for some particular *shibboleth* of our own. We are only to stand like this about great, vital, central matters of doctrine. There are matters about which Christian people have never agreed. We must not, for example, use this kind of language for odd points of prophecy or if a man does not take our particular prophetic view; the New Testament does not make this stand on matters like that. No, but on central doctrine, this is where we have to walk carefully and circumspectly. So we are not only to draw the distinction between ourselves and the truth, but also between truth which is central and of which we must be certain, and matters about which there may be what we can describe as a legitimate difference of opinion. So the point here is that John does regard this particular matter clearly as of central and vital importance. That is why he not only uses this language but makes such a strong appeal.

Let us, then, consider it like this: Why is John so concerned about this matter? Why does he call these antichrists liars? Why does he say that these people who are teaching that the eternal Son of God came upon the man Jesus at the baptism and left Him on the Cross–why does he say that such people are liars–why does he denounce them so vehemently? There are a number of answers to that question. The first is that what the antichrists are saying is a lie, and he goes on to elaborate: 'Who is a liar but he that denieth that Jesus is the Christ? He is antichrist, that denieth the Father and the Son.' John has already said, 'I have not written unto you because ye know not the truth, but because ye know it, and that no lie is of the truth' (v 21). And that is his first reason–that what these people were teaching does not correspond to the facts.

We can put it like this: John has already said that the essence of his preaching is based upon what he has seen with his eyes–'which we have looked upon, and our hands have handled, of the Word of life' (1:1). He says, 'For the life was manifested . . . that which was from the beginning' (1-21). 'Now,' says John in effect, 'these people are denying certain facts of which I am a witness and about which I can testify–they are liars.' He has been reminding us, in other words, that he and the other Apostles had been with the Lord on the Mount of Transfiguration. Peter, James and John were there, and they saw and heard the conversation and the testimony; they even heard the voice from heaven which said, 'This is my beloved Son, in whom I am well pleased; hear ye him' (Matt 17:5). 'So what these people teach,' says John, 'is a contradiction of what the voice of God has said; it is a lie, and what else can you say about it?'

'To say that the eternal Christ left the man Jesus on the cross and that it was only the man Jesus who died is a lie,' says John, 'I was there–I saw the Son of God die. I was in the upper room when He said to Thomas, "Reach hither thy finger, and behold my hands," and when He said to all of us, "A spirit hath not flesh and bones as ye see me have; a spirit cannot eat as you see me eating." I am a witness of these things. I am here to testify that it was the Son of God who died, and we saw Him ascending into heaven after His resurrection.' So there is a sense in which we say that there is nothing else to be said about such teaching except to brand it as a lie. It is not true; it is a denial of the facts; it is a denial of God's own testimony to His only begotten Son who came here on earth.

Now to put that in its modern form, take all these attempts, so-called, during the last hundred years to reconstruct 'the Jesus of history'–attempts to get rid of the miracles and the supernatural element. It seems to me that there is only one thing to say about all this–it is not true, it is a lie, it is a monstrosity. Look at these attempts of the liberals to reconstruct Jesus–that is not the person I see in the New Testament, that is not the Saviour of my soul. What they have produced is something unreal; it does not correspond to the facts. You cannot explain the New Testament in that way; you cannot explain the history of the Church like that; so John denounces it, because it is nothing but a simple departure from the truth.

Furthermore, I wonder whether we will not all agree that it would have been a better thing not only for the Christian Church but also for the world perhaps if our fathers and our grandfathers had faced this false teaching which came from Germany, this subtle attempt to reconstruct Jesus. Would it not have been better if they had faced it and branded it as a lie instead of trying to accommodate to it and to fit it in–instead of all this false spirit of toleration which is such a striking departure from that which we see characterised the apostles, and even the Lord Himself, in His teaching. That is the first thing the Apostle has to say.

Then secondly, John warns these people against this subtle danger and urges them to avoid it because of certain consequences which follow from believing it. It is not only untrue in and of itself, but consider these consequences: 'He is antichrist, that denieth the Father and the Son. Whosoever denieth the Son, the same hath not the Father; but he that acknowledgeth the Son hath the Father also.' Let me split that up a certain way. Here are the consequences of accepting this false teaching.

It first of all involves a denial of the real nature of the person of the Lord Jesus Christ. It denies the Son, says John; in other words, it denies the very doctrine of the Incarnation. If this false teaching which John is denouncing is true, then everything that is described in Philippians 2 is not true either–that great passage where Paul speaks of Him who was 'in the form of God' and 'thought it not robbery to be equal with God.' The divesting Himself of the insignia of His glory and being here in this world in the fashion of a man, taking the form of a servant and so on–all that is then not true. The Incarnation is no longer a fact; the glory and the marvel and the mystery of the birth and death is just a fairy tale. Jesus as a babe in the manger is just a human being and no more; there is no such thing as the virgin birth or the miraculous. He was just an ordinary child like every other child. And then, it is said, upon that child grown man at the baptism by John in the Jordan, there descended the eternal Christ who came for a while and influenced

Him, raised Him up above Himself and then left Him upon the cross!

No! This is a denial of the whole doctrine of the Incarnation, which is most central in the New Testament. You no longer have the God-man, all these things are not true and one of the central glories of the gospel is lost.

But not only that–you see, of course, that at the same time it also makes some of the other most essential parts of the gospel history quite untrue; the agony in the Garden becomes very unreal if this teaching is right, and the Son of God no longer died upon the cross; the most amazing thing that the world has ever seen really did not happen. Well, we need not delay with this; you see immediately that it is a denial of the doctrine of the two natures in one person, that amazing truth which is central and vital in this New Testament teaching.

But let me go on to point out that it not only denies the person–it also denies the work of Christ, and it does so in this way. 'Who is a liar but he that denieth that Jesus is the Christ?' What or who is '*the Christ*'? He is the Anointed One, who has been set apart by God to do a certain work. And what the New Testament teaches is that Jesus, the Son of God, was set apart by his Father and anointed with the Holy Spirit without measure in order to do that work. What was that work? It was the work of saving mankind; it was the work of taking the sins of the world upon Him, of suffering and bearing our punishment to make reconciliation for us; and then rising again to be our representative and advocate and to stand in heaven on our behalf.

So it is obviously a denial of that if the Son of God left the man Jesus. Where is the atonement? The only one who could make atonement must be the Eternal Himself. No man could do it; it is only the Son of God who can bear the sins of the whole world. So if He left the man Jesus upon the cross, there is no atonement; you and I are still in our sins; we are still under the law; we are still under the wrath of God; there is no forgiveness for us, and we are truly undone and lost.

Are you surprised now that John called these people 'liars'? Is it surprising that he brands that teaching as a lie? Anything that robs me of my salvation and my standing with God is a lie, and I must denounce it with all my being. It is a denial of the person and of the work of the Lord Jesus Christ.

But John does not stop at that; he goes on to say that anyone who denies the doctrine concerning God the Father is a liar: 'Who is a liar but he that denieth that Jesus is the Christ? He is antichrist, that denieth the Father and the Son. Whosoever denieth the Son, the same hath not the Father: but he that acknowledgeth the Son hath the Father also.'

Now this is very high doctrine, but you remember that our Lord Himself has already indicated the same truth in the fifth chapter of John's Gospel. What it really amounts to is this: there is no real doctrine of the Father, and of God, except in terms of the Lord Jesus Christ. Our Lord also said, 'I am the way, the truth, and the life: no man cometh unto the Father, but by me' (John 14:6). So if we deny the person of Jesus Christ, we do not know the Father—we have lost Him. We may be living with some vague belief in God as a power or force or someone who can help us in a moment of need, but the teaching of our Lord Himself, as it is the teaching of all the New Testament Apostles, is that there is no such thing as a true knowledge of God apart from the Lord Jesus Christ.

You can believe in a creator, you can believe in some unseen influence, but you will never know the Father except in the Son. 'He that hath seen me,' said our Lord, 'hath seen the Father' (John 14:9). So to deny the Son is to deny the Father; we do not know God as Father except in and through the Lord Jesus Christ. That is why John calls this other teaching a lie; that is why he brands these people as liars. They are not only robbing me of the Son, they are robbing me of the Father also, and I am left in the old position of vaguely groping in the dark trying to find God.

Let me put this in another way. I not only lose the Father from the doctrinal standpoint, I lose one of the greatest comforts that the gospel has to offer me. Do you remember those tender words which our Lord spoke to His disciples and the Pharisees when He taught them how to pray? He said, 'Your heavenly Father knoweth that ye have need of all these things' (Matt 6:32), and He told them that the very hairs of their head were all numbered (Matt 10:30), and that God is our Father in that sense. But if this other teaching is right, then God is not my Father, and I am left to myself with a God whom I fear in the distance, some almighty terrible power. To deny the Son is also to deny the Father, whom I can only know truly through the Son; and therefore the great comfort that John offers these Christians–that of fellowship with the Father and with His Son, Jesus Christ–is not true. And if that is not true, what have I as a Christian in a world like this? Where is my joy to come from; how can I stand the forces that are set against me? The very basis of his epistle has gone, and hence his strong language.

But there is one further step. This false teaching not only denies the person of the Son and of the Father, it therefore of necessity denies the doctrine of the Trinity. It is only as we believe the truth concerning Jesus of Nazareth as the Son of God that we really arrive at our doctrine of the Trinity at all. It is He who opens the door to an understanding of this ultimate doctrine of the Christian faith. I do not know about the Father until I know the Son; and it is when I know the Father and the Son that I begin to understand the doctrine of the Holy Spirit who is sent by the Father and the Son and who, as it were, is there with the Father and the Son and explains the intimate relationship between them.

I lose everything if I deny the doctrine of the Son. It is the eternal Father who has planned salvation; it is the Son who came and worked out that plan; and it is God the Holy Spirit who opens our eyes to it and who makes it real and actual in us all. So you see why John is concerned about all these matters, because to deny this central aspect is to rob us of all the glorious doctrine of our Christian faith. To deny the Son is to deny the Father, and to deny the Father and the Son is to deny the Holy Spirit; so we are left to ourselves with our human wisdom and understanding and philosophy and our own vain efforts and endeavours to try to find God. No, says John, this is a lie, and it leads to such consequences.

But lastly, just a word on John's third ground of appeal, which is the consequences of believing the truth. We have just been looking at the consequences of believing the lie, but, says John, 'I would not stop at that. Let me show you the consequences of believing the truth.' 'And this is the promise that he hath promised us, even eternal life.' 'Beloved people,' says John in effect, 'don't believe the lie. It not only robs you of the doctrine, it robs you of life; it is that which robs you of God's greatest gift which has been made possible by the incarnation of His Son. If the eternal Son had not come from God and been made flesh, if there is no union between human nature and the Son of God, how can I have a new nature? I cannot be born again, because to be born again means to receive the nature of Christ, and if the nature of Christ is unreal, if there is only the coming of the Son of God upon the man Jesus and then His leaving him, there is no union, and therefore the rebirth is impossible. But that is the wondrous thing that is offered and is possible to me. It is the very thing that God does promise us, even eternal life.'

And then the final thing is that which John emphasises in verse 28: 'And now, little children, abide in him; that, when he shall appear, we may have confidence, and not be ashamed before him, at his coming.' 'Don't believe that lie,' says John in effect, 'because if you do, you will find yourself face to face with it as a fact. These people have denied the truth,' says John, 'they think they are being clever. They have this mixture of philosophy and mysticism, and they have been trying to make us believe in a kind of phantom body and that the eternal God came upon a man and then left him. It is unreal,' says John, 'don't believe it. The day is coming when you will face the fact–the God-man is coming into this world. He will come again, and then you will see Him; and if you believe that lie, you will be ashamed when you see Him.'

Writing in the Apocalypse, John says, 'Every eye shall see him, and they also which pierced him' (Rev 1:7). And when they see Him they will cry out 'to the mountains and rocks, Fall on us, and hide us . . . from the wrath of the Lamb' (Rev 6:16). This is a fact; this is not fancy. The God-Man will come again, and if you want to rejoice in that day, if you want to have confidence when you look at Him, and if you want to say, 'Even so come, Lord Jesus,' then avoid this lie, beware of these seducers, these liars who deny that Jesus is the Christ, and hold on to the truth. Let the truth abide in you, for if it does, that great day of His appearing will not come to you as a surprise. It will not come as a shock or as a condemnation;

you will not be offended and ashamed; no, you will rejoice in it, you will glory in it, and you will stand with confidence and look into His holy face.

That is the argument of the Apostle. The false teaching is a lie; it leads to those terrible consequences, and it robs us of the blessed consequences of believing the truth of the rebirth and regeneration, of new life from God and that blessed hope of His appearing, the truth of the new heaven and the new earth in which dwells righteousness, in which we shall be with Him for ever.

# NOTES

*CHAPTER ONE: Sin*

1. This sermon was preached on Sunday, January 2nd, 1949.
2. Cf. *Fellowship with God*, Vol. 1 of this series (Crossway, 1992).

*CHAPTER THREE: The Advocate*

1. Cf. *Fellowship with God*, Vol. 1 of this series (Crossway, 1992).

*CHAPTER SIX: Children, Young Men, and Fathers*

1. For a detailed discussion of these verses, see *Fellowship with God*, Vol. 1 of this series (Crossway, 1992).

*CHAPTER EIGHT: The Antichrist*

1. Cf. *Fellowship with God*, Vol. 1 of this series (Crossway, 1992).